TABLE OF CONTENTS

Page

MASTER OF MILITARY ART AND SCIENCE THESIS APPROVAL PAGE iii

ABSTRACT.. iv

ACKNOWLEDGMENTS v

TABLE OF CONTENTS... vi

ACRONYMS ix

TABLES x

CHAPTER 1 INTRODUCTION 1

   Introduction and Background 1
   Statement of the Problem/Purpose of the Study 5
   Research Question 6
   Definition of Terms 6
   Limitation of Scope and Delimitations 8
   Assumptions... 9
   Significance of Thesis.. 9

CHAPTER 2 LITERATURE REVIEW 12

   The Purpose of the Research 12
   Description of Chapter Two 12
   Insurgency Literature 13
   Field Manual 3-24, *Counterinsurgency* 14
   Lieutenant Colonel David Galula 17
   Dr. Bard O'Neill 18
   Mexican Drug Cartels... 19
   Mexican Political History 20

CHAPTER 3 RESEARCH METHODOLOGY 24

   The Purpose of the Research 24
   The Organization of Chapter Three 24
   Data Collection 25
   The Method 26
   Limitations 27

CHAPTER 4 ANALYSIS 29

Introduction to Chapter Four 29
Mexican History 30
  Introduction.. 30
  The Separatist Traditions of Mexico.. 32
  The Haciendas System 33
  Labor Conditions Prior to the Revolution.. 37
  The Cananea Consolidated Copper Company 38
  The Rio Blanco Textile Mills... 39
  President Jose de la Cruz Porfirio Diaz Mori 40
  The Revolution Begins 41
  1920 to 2006 42
  The Transformation from Haciendas to Cartel 44
  Increased Violence 47
The Definition of Insurgency 49
  The Dynamics of Insurgency 52
    Introduction to the Dynamics of Insurgency 52
    Types of Insurgency's and Their Causes 55
    The Problem in Mexico 57
    The Criminal Element and External Support...................................... 59
    The Ideology 61
    The Objectives 62
    The Strategic Objective... 62
    The Operational and Tactical Objectives.. 63
    The Organization 65
  Elements of an Insurgency.. 66
    The Movement Leader... 67
    The Combatants 68
    The Political Cadre 69
    The Auxiliaries.. 72
    The Mass Base 73
  The Scope of the Network 74
  Chapter Four Conclusions... 77

CHAPTER 5 CONCLUSIONS AND RECOMMENDATIONS 85

Introduction to Chapter Five... 85
Summary of Chapter Four 86
What Does this Mean for Mexico? 88
What Does this Mean for the United States?... 89
  Increased Flow of Narcotics and Funding 90
  Increase in Violence Along the Border and in Major U.S. Cities........... 92
Vulnerabilities of the Narco-Insurgency.. 94
Recommendations.. 97
Support from the United States.. 99

For Future Study 101
The U.S. Military Officer and the Narco-insurgency 101

BIBLIOGRAPHY 105

ACRONYMS

AFI   Federal Investigative Agency

CI   Counterinsurgency

CJCS   Chairman, Joint Chiefs of Staff

COIN   Counterinsurgency

DOJ   Department of Justice

DSCA   Department of Defense Support to Civilian Authorities

FAS   Federation of American Scientists

GAFES   Grupo Aeromovil de Fuerzas Especiales (Special Forces Airmobile Group)

GWOT   Global War on Terror

LOC   Lines of Communication

MS-13   Mara Salvatrucha

NAFTA   North American Free Trade Agreement

PRI   Institutional Revolutionary Party

SSI   Strategic Studies Institute

USAID   United States Agency for International Development

TABLES

Page

Table 1. Dynamics of Insurgency 54

Table 2. Elements of Insurgency...67

CHAPTER 1

INTRODUCTION

Introduction and Background

A war is raging in Mexico. It is a narco-insurgency that threatens the legitimacy of the Mexican government. This is not a new conflict however, the recent spikes in violence between the Mexican cartels and Mexican law enforcement have increased to levels that have government officials, military officials, and the public, in both United States and Mexico, gravely concerned. Recently, the Mexican President Felipe Calderon, when asked to comment about the drug situation in Mexico admitted, ―It's a war."[1]

In addition to the threat of increased violence, the strategic concern about the narco-insurgency centers around the increasing capabilities of the cartels. The internal organizations that make up the narco-insurgency possess the capability to create a powerful ‗shadow government' to the government of Mexico through infiltration of the government bureaucracy and growing public support. These intentions are reinforced by recent reports that demonstrate the cartels capacity for and willingness to use violence in the pursuit of their goals of expanding their political control throughout Mexico. Reports such as the 9 September 2010 Associated Press (AP) article that noted the fact that, ―a third mayor in a month was slain by suspected drug gang hit men,"[2] within northern Mexico.

The war against the drug cartels within Mexico is quickly exhausting the resources of the Mexican government. This is evident by the recent deployment of Mexican federal police and military to numerous locations across Mexico to fill a void where local authorities have become ineffective. The *Los Angeles Times* reported that,

Mexican President Calderon has deployed 45,000 troops and 5,000 federal police to 18 states, where trafficking groups are fighting local authorities and battling for access to the U.S. [drug] market."[3] The Mexican government understands the seriousness and extent of the threat posed by the cartels and has even gone as far as to recruit a, top Salvadoran ex-guerrilla commander,"[4] to advise President Calderon on how to use military tactics to increase pressure on the drug cartels.

The drug cartels in Mexico are organized, effective, and are attempting to neutralize the Mexican government in order to continue drug trafficking operations unabated. The *New York Times* reported that, While Mr. Calderon dismisses suggestions that Mexico is a failed state, he and his aides have spoken frankly of the cartels' attempts to set up a state within a state, levying taxes, throwing up roadblocks and enforcing their own perverse code of behavior."[5] Characteristic of an insurgency, the drug cartels have also assumed control of the media. Out of fear for violent retribution from the cartels, many news organizations along the U.S.-Mexican border refuse to report on the drug issues within their viewing or listening area. *The New York Times* reported that, Acts against news organizations in 2010 have included the kidnapping of four journalists, who were released after one station broadcasted videos as demanded by that of their abductors, and a car bomb detonating in August outside a regional office of Televisa, the leading national network."[6] These scare tactics used by the drug cartels are very much like the actions characteristic of an insurgency. These tactics aim to create widespread fear, to increase and maintain the cartels control over towns and areas within Mexico while preventing local law enforcement from interfering with their operations.

The astronomical profits the drug cartels collect are based on an ever increasing demand for drugs in the U.S. As the drug cartels get richer, the Mexican and U.S. governments are spending billions of dollars each year to conduct counter drug operations throughout each country and to secure the border region. Current estimates claim that each of the major drug cartels collect billions of dollars in profits from the distribution of narcotics and use this money to fund multiple subordinate gangs who support their operations by helping to maintain and secure multiple avenues into and out of the U.S. for drug smuggling. The current violence within Mexico is a result of the drug cartels and their supporting street gangs fighting against rival cartels and, in most cases, against the government. These fights are not petty gang fights but are for the control of ‒billions of dollars in profits from tons of smuggled marijuana, and other drugs, and the precious control of Mexican border cities like Ciudad Juarez; Nogales; and Tijuana. Those cities are thoroughfares to the world's most lucrative drug market: the United States."[7]

As the Mexican Army quickly mobilizes to combat this growing threat that has engulfed their country, the U.S. prepares for what is sure to be a tidal wave of similar drug activity within our borders. Once drugs are moved across the US-Mexico border they are distributed to different gangs that quickly move the drugs using an equally complex and integrated network across the U.S. This network, established by the sales of narcotics from Mexico, has an almost unlimited scope throughout the U.S. and Canada.

Along the national border, cities, and towns have been plagued with an influx of gangs who stay locked in a constant battle between themselves and U.S. law enforcement agencies, for the control of territory for the transportation of their narcotics. Gang related

3

tactics range from a combination of digging underground tunnels, dropping caches, and using vehicles to get people and drugs cross the border. The U.S. Coast Guard has observed and interdicted drug cartels using high speed boats, submersibles, and low flying cargo planes to move drugs across the open waters of the Gulf of Mexico. As law enforcement agencies have increased their presence along the border, drug cartels have resorted to using insurgent type operations to create instability within local governments thereby preventing a unified and coordinated effort by law enforcement to interdict their drug trafficking operations.

In December of 2009, when researching the vast area that the drug cartels control, *The New York Times* discovered that U.S. law enforcement officials have identified, ―230 cities, including Anchorage, Atlanta, Boston and Billings, Montana,‖[8] where Mexican drug cartels and their affiliates ―maintain drug distribution networks or supply drugs to distributors,‖[9] According to the Department of Justice (DoJ), in a statement made that same year, the number of cities with drug cartel activity rose from 100 cities reported three years earlier, although DoJ officials said that may be because of better data collection methods as well as the spread of the organizations.[10] With alarming reports that depict the extended reach of the cartels into the U.S., the issue of the long, mostly unguarded, southwestern border of the U.S. is rapidly becoming a heavily debated topic during discussions of the vulnerabilities posing a threat to homeland security.

In recent efforts to assist the Mexican government in their fight against the cartels and the drug trafficking network, the U.S. recently sent U.S. Navy Admiral. Mike Mullen, the Chairman of the Joint Chiefs of Staff (CJCS), to confer with Mexican leaders. Adm. Mullen informed the Mexican government about the U.S. governments‗

extension of the Merida Initiative, a three year-plan signed into law last June to flood the U.S.-Mexican border region with $1.4 billion in U.S. assistance for law-enforcement training and equipment, as well as technical advice and training to bolster Mexico's judicial system."[11]

Statement of the Problem/Purpose of the Study

The purpose of this research is to determine if the operations, actions, and activities being conducted by the various Mexican drug cartels, with support from their network of street gangs and individuals from the lower class of Mexican society, qualifies as an insurgency as defined by a combination of the U.S. Army's Field Manual (FM) 3-24, *Counterinsurgency,* and other counterinsurgency references. This research will show that the cartels are waging what is commonly referred to as narco-insurgency using a combination of political and social influences to achieve their strategic goals of continuing to acquire income from unlimited, illegal economic profits. This research will show that the root causes and support for this insurgency stem from long term social inequalities between the different social classes within Mexican society. This will be done by examining historical events and long lasting social and economic issues within Mexico while framing the present situation with the most current insurgency and counterinsurgency doctrine. This research will also provide recommendations for the Mexican government to consider while combating this narco-insurgency along with possible support functions the U.S. can perform to aid Mexico in their fight.

Research Question

In order to determine if the drug trafficking situation in Mexico is now an insurgency and no longer simply a law enforcement issue, and to make credible recommendations, the author developed and answered several research questions. The primary question of this paper asks: Are the drug cartels and their network of supporting street gangs an insurgency within Mexico?

To successfully address the primary research question, the author must also answer six secondary questions:

1. What is an insurgency?

2. Do the elements and dynamics of the drug cartels within Mexico parallel those of an insurgency?

3. What social, economic, and political factors influence and support the drug trafficking operations within Mexico?

4. What implications does the narco-insurgency have on the U.S. and Mexican governments?

5. What actions should the Mexican government take to control the narco-insurgency?

6. What actions can the U.S. government take to interdict drug trafficking along the border and what support can the U.S. provide to the Mexican government?

Definition of Terms

Terms defined as part of this thesis are described below. These are the manner in which these terms are used within the context of this thesis.

Counterinsurgency: Those military, paramilitary, political, economic, psychological, and civic actions taken by a government to defeat an insurgency.[12]

Drug/Narcotics Manufacturing: The act of creating illegal narcotics by combining legal substances or strengthening the effects of the natural ingredients. In this research manufacturing narcotics includes packaging narcotics for trafficking and smuggle operations within Mexico.

Drug/Narcotics Production: The act of growing the natural ingredients necessary for the production of narcotics.

Drug-Smuggling: The act of secretly transporting narcotics across the U.S. Mexico border.

Drug-Trafficking/Narco-Trafficking: The act of transporting drugs or narcotics between locations within Mexico and the United States.

Homeland defense: Joint doctrine defines homeland defense as the protection of United States sovereignty, territory, domestic population, and critical infrastructure against external threats and aggression or other threats as directed by the President.[13]

Homeland security: Joint doctrine defines homeland security as a concerted national effort to prevent terrorist attacks within the United States; reduce America's vulnerability to terrorism, major disasters, and other emergencies; and minimize the damage and recover from attacks, major disasters, and other emergencies that occur.[14]

Host Nation: A nation that receives the forces and or supplies of allied nations, coalition partners, and or NATO organizations to be located on, to operate in, or to transit through its territory.[15]

Insurgency: An organized movement aimed at the overthrow of a constitutional government through the use of subversion and armed conflict.[16]

Narco-Insurgency: An organization that possesses the capability to use violence and the other necessary resources to wage a protracted struggle whose operational objective is to delegitimize the control of an established government in attempts to secure their strategic objective of unrestricted narcotics operations and other illegal markets for economic profit.

Limitation of Scope and Delimitations

This research is limited to analyzing the general characteristics of the Mexican cartels as a whole and using examples of specific cartels to illustrate points. This research also remains focused on the overall effects the narco-insurgency is having on the Mexican government instead of just focusing on the most politically threatening or most violent cartels. The history of Mexico provided in this research spans decades and is only meant to be an overview of major events along the timeline leading up to the present day situation in Mexico as related to the cartels and the major causes that fuel gang participation and recruitment. This research also intentionally limited the amount of counterinsurgency and insurgency references in order to focus primarily on the U.S. Army's new FM 3-24, *Counterinsurgency*, due to the relevance and current notoriety of the manual, and in order to limit the vast theories and fluid characteristics indicative to an insurgency to a manageable number.

Assumptions

Due to the illegal nature of the drug cartels, their actual goals and true ideologies are somewhat secret. Therefore, connections between the drug cartels and the supporting network of gangs is assumed to be based on monetary profit and agreed upon loyalties. This research assumes that the situation between the Mexican government and the drug cartels will continue to increase in violence. This research also assumes that the Mexican government is not a ―failed state" and still possesses the capability to effectively direct counterinsurgency efforts against the cartels.

This research assumed that FM 3-24 is an accurate counterinsurgency manual and conveys an accurate definition and description of insurgency based on its numerous contributors, widespread staffing and coordination to include international collaboration. This research also assumes that FM 3-24 provides a common conceptual framework and set of principals, terms, and ideas applicable across all military and government agencies providing a standard lexicon for officials to use as reference when discussing counterinsurgency.

Significance of Thesis

Securing our nation's borders is a top priority for the current administration however; the solution to the threat along the southwestern border continues to evade government and military officials at both state and national levels. This priority is reinforced by the May *2010 National Security Strategy* (*NSS*):

> We will continue to rebalance our military capabilities to excel at counterterrorism, counterinsurgency, stability operations, and meeting increasingly sophisticated security threats, while ensuring our force is ready to address deterring and defeating aggression in anti-access environments, and defending the United States and supporting civil authorities at home.[17]

This statement from the NSS demonstrates that present and future military officers need to be prepared to conduct counterinsurgency, counterterrorism, and defeat sophisticated security threats while defending the U.S. and supporting civilian authorities. Nowhere else in America is the threat to homeland security greater than along the southwestern border. Evidence shows the situation in Mexico is continuing to deteriorate, while the threat of violence is growing, and narco-insurgency bloodshed is increasing the potential for ―spilling over" violence along the border posing a considerable threat to the safety of U.S. citizens living in the area.

The significance of this research aims to enlighten U.S. government and military officials to the situation the Mexican government is currently facing as they continue to battle the drug cartels for control of their country. This research will also provide recommendations for officials to consider when designing initiatives to control the narco-insurgency within Mexico. Chapter 2 of this research will provide a review of the literature detailing information about Mexican history, insurgency, counterinsurgency, and the situation surrounding the drug cartels and their supporting network of gangs.

---

[1] ―Mexico Under Siege: The drug war at our doorstep," *Los Angeles Times,* http://projects.latimes.com/mexico-drug-war/#/its-a-war (accessed 17 October, 2010).

[2] Mark Stevenson, ―Clinton: Mexican Drug Cartels Like ‗Insurgency,'" *Fox News,* 9 September 2010, http://www.foxnews.com/world/2010/09/08/mexican-mayor-killed-marines-arrest-suspects-massacre-migrants/ (accessed 17 October 2010).

[3] *Los Angeles Times,* 17 October 2010.

[4] Tracy Wilkinson, ―A Top Salvadoran Ex-guerrilla Commander Advised Mexico's Conservative President," *Los Angeles Times,* 22 October 2010, http://www.latimes.com/news/nationworld/world/la-fg-mexico-guru-20101023,0,7109037.story (accessed 17 October 2010).

[5] ―Mexican Drug Trafficking,‖ *The New York Times,* 21 October 2010, http://topics.nytimes.com/top/news/international/countriesandterritories/mexico/drug_trafficking/index.html?scp=1&sq=mexican%20drug%20cartels&st=cse (accessed 17 October 2010).

[6] Ibid.

[7] Solomon Moore, ―How U.S. Became Stage for Mexican Drug Feud,‖ *The New York Times*, 8 December 2009, http://www.nytimes.com/2009/12/09/us/09border.html (accessed 17 October 2010).

[8] ―Mexican Drug Cartel Violence Spills Over, Alarming U.S.,‖ *The New York Times,* 22 March 2009, http://www.nytimes.com/2009/03/23/us/23border.html (accessed 17 October 2010).

[9] Ibid.

[10] Ibid.

[11] Alex Johnson, ―In Mexico's drug wars, fears of U.S. front,‖ *MSNBC,* 9 March 2009, http://www.msnbc.msn.com/id/29516551/ (accessed 17 October 2010).

[12] U.S. Department of the Army, Field Manual (FM) 3-24, *Counterinsurgency* (Washington, D.C: Government Printing Office, 2006), Glossary 4.

[13] U.S. Department of Defense, Joint Publication (JP) 3-27, *Homeland Defense* (Washington, DC: Government Printing Office, 2007), vii.

[14] U.S. Department of Defense, Joint Publication (JP) 3-28, *Civil Support* (Washington, DC: Government Printing Office, 2007), GL-8.

[15] U.S. Department of Defense, FM 3-24, *Counterinsurgency,* Glossary-5.

[16] Ibid. Glossary-5.

[17] The White House, *The National Security Strategy of the United States of America* (Washington, DC: Government Printing Office, 2010), 14.

CHAPTER 2

LITERATURE REVIEW

The Purpose of the Research

The purpose of this research is to determine if the operations, actions, and activities being conducted by the various Mexican drug cartels, with support from their network of street gangs and individuals from the lower class of Mexican society, qualifies as an insurgency as defined by a combination of the U.S. Army's Field Manual (FM) 3-24, *Counterinsurgency,* and other counterinsurgency references. This research will show that the cartels are waging a narco-insurgency using a combination of political and social influence to achieve their strategic goals of continuing to earn income from unlimited illegal economic profits. This research will show that the root causes and support for this insurgency stem from long term inequalities between the social classes within Mexico. This will be done by examining historical events and long lasting social and economic issues within Mexico while framing the situation with the most current insurgency and or counterinsurgency doctrine.

This research will also provide recommendations for the Mexican government to consider while combating this narco-insurgency along with possible support functions the U.S. can perform to aid Mexico in their fight.

Description of Chapter Two

Chapter 2 is organized by topic. In this research, in order to understand the narco-insurgency the Mexican government is facing, one must first gather the tools and literature that provide the background and insight into Mexican political, social, and economic history and the evolution of drug trafficking between the U.S. and Mexico. In addition to understanding Mexico itself, there is also a need for references that provide insight into the world of an insurgency which will provide this research with a framework or lens through which to view the situation in Mexico.

In chapter 2, this research will first describe the literature used in developing a definition for the term insurgency and outline the elements and dynamics indicative of an insurgency. Second, this research will analyze the literature that show the evolution of the drug cartels, and how government oppression coupled with the growing separation between the classes has created an environment where the majority of the Mexican population feels as if they have no other alternative to better their lives than to believe in the social and economic promises offered by the drug cartels and gang lifestyle.

Third, this research will discuss the references used to analyze the general elements and dynamics of the drug cartels and gangs, their narco-trafficking activities and insurgency operations, and the affect these operations are having on the central government of Mexico.

Insurgency Literature

To dissect the complex phenomenon of insurgency, this research chose three main resources. The first is the U.S. Army's recently published Field Manuel (FM) 3-24, *Counterinsurgency*, published in December of 2006, at the height of U.S. involvement in The Global War on Terrorism. This manual was produced to fill a gap in U.S. Army doctrine, which up until that point had previously been focused mainly on high intensity warfare involving major combat operations but little on insurgency and even less on counterinsurgency. This manual contain doctrine that was badly needed to assist U.S.

forces who, at the time, were decisively engaged fighting insurgencies on two separate fronts in Iraq and Afghanistan.

The second source is LTC David Galula's book titled, *Counterinsurgency Warfare: Theory and Practice,* originally published in 1964. LTC Galula was a French Officer who participated in conventional warfare within North Africa, Italy, and France and faced insurgencies within China, Greece, Indochina, and Algeria. His book, *Counterinsurgency Warfare,* is a collection of his personal experiences and research on the subject. He is one of the many leading insurgency experts that are referenced in FM 3-24, *Counterinsurgency*.

The third insurgency focused literature resource is Dr. Bard O'Neill's book titled, *Insurgency and Terrorism: From Revolution to Apocalypse,* published in 2005. A professor of international affairs at the National War College in, Washington, D.C. O'Neill is the Director of Studies of Insurgency and Revolution. O'Neill has also been consulted on numerous occasions by the Department of State (DoS) and Department of Defense (DoD) on issues concerning Israel, Egypt, Jordan, Saudi Arabia, Iran, and other countries.

Field Manual 3-24, *Counterinsurgency*

The U.S. Army's recently published FM 3-24, *Counterinsurgency,* is a vital and unique resource due to its currency, the fact that it was researched and written simultaneously as the U.S. was engaged in fighting two separate and unique insurgencies, and that the manual was developed by combining the views and opinions of many different insurgency and counterinsurgency experts and theorists. This fusing of ideas from many of the leading experts, past and present, produced a reference that, upon close examination, appears to contain an accurate and encompassing spectrum of insurgency and counterinsurgency material. This manual uses historical examples, provides general descriptions and prescriptions, and references numerous insurgency experts, while taking into account the reality of modern warfare in its influence on the insurgent organization. This will be useful in framing the situation in Mexico and providing recommendations for modern counterinsurgency tactics that both the government of Mexico and the U.S. can utilize. This is not to say that FM 3-24, *Counterinsurgency* is perfect as it does have its critics; however it currently provides the most reliable resource for reference and study on the fundamentals, characteristics and principles of modern insurgency and counterinsurgency.

Military officers and government officials who are dissatisfied with the manual claim that the terms and definitions within FM 3-24 are, ‟too general" in nature. This might be true however, for those who have had a great deal of experience doing research on specific insurgencies or operated within a unit conducting counterinsurgency operations will agree that due to the fluid and evolving world of insurgency, these general terms can be helpful. Any effort to develop specific terms that identify all the elements of a single insurgency and evenly apply it to every historical or future insurgency would be fruitless, since no two insurgencies are exactly the same. This is why general terms are beneficial to the counterinsurgent organization, and to this research, since they provide a common framework of structure of themes, elements, and dynamics inherent in the majority of insurgencies.

An example of the criticism for using doctrine like FM 3-24 to make generalizations about counterinsurgencies is noted by Mr. Matthew Lauder, in his book titled, *Religion and Resistance: Examining the Role of Religion in Irregular Warfare,* where he states, ―The primary concern of the critics is that, by over-generalizing the various forms of insurgency, and by developing secular theories of violence (based largely on the communist revolutions of the twentieth century), contemporary counter-insurgency doctrine ignores the distinctive and unique qualities of conflict defined, framed, and driven by religion."[1]

Lauder has a valid point however, the primary focus of FM 3-24, *Counterinsurgency* is not to identify and inform combat soldiers and leaders about specific insurgencies, but instead, to assist government, military, and law enforcement personnel in conducting counterinsurgency operations by outlining broad, common trends within historic insurgencies. This way, units and leaders conducting counterinsurgency operations can utilize the manual in multiple scenarios without trying to specifically match the description or characteristics of a specific type insurgency to the present conditions they face.

Another critic from military and official government circles concerning FM 3-24 centers on a perception that manual lacks discussion of the application of kinetic effects and combat fighting. An example of this type of critic comes from LTC Gian P. Gentile, the former commander of the U.S. Army's 8-10 Armored Cavalry Reconnaissance Squadron, who commanded the squadron in western Baghdad in 2006. Gentile states in his article, ―Our COIN Doctrine Removes the Enemy from the Essence of War," that, ―My basic argument in *Eating soup with a spoon* was that the theoretical premise of the manual embodied in Chapter 1's various paradoxes, specifically two emblematic ones, removed the essence of war—fighting—from its pages."[2]

Gentiles comment is valid however, one paradox he fails to take into account is the one that states, ‑having superior fire power, maneuver, or strength does not guarantee you success when fighting an insurgency and in some cases can benefit the insurgent rather than the counterinsurgent." What this means is the omission of discussion on kinetic combat from FM 3-24 may have been intentional since the major objectives in COIN operations are normally more psychological in nature and generally involve the population in terms of their will and popular support rather than traditional objectives we are more accustomed too that are either terrain or enemy based. Critics like Gentile are important, but their argument is questionable in defeating an insurgency. Chapter 5 of this research will also discuss different objectives and approaches to defeating the narco-insurgency in Mexico. These objectives and the approaches discussed will involve addressing social and economic problems instead of relying solely attacking the drug cartels and their affiliated gangs.

<u>Lieutenant Colonel David Galula</u>

In order to better understand the roots of FM 3-24, *Counterinsurgency*, this research will analyze the work by one of the largest contributors to the manual, LTC David Galula. As stated previously, Galula was an experienced French Officer who fought and studied insurgencies within China, Greece, Indochina, and Algeria. During his lifetime, Galula was invited to participate in many symposiums intended to advise civilian leaders on the topic of counterinsurgency. In his book, *Counterinsurgency Warfare: Theory and Practice,* published in 1964, Galula addresses the common characteristics and vulnerabilities he found in the various insurgencies and recommends steps for civil and military leaders to follow in an effort to control the threat of an insurgency within their country. Based on this researcher's recent combat experience, it is readily apparent from those experiences that many of the lessons that Galula outlines in his book continue to have relevance and application in COIN operations the U.S. is conducting within Iraq and Afghanistan today. No doubt, this publication is one of the great counterinsurgency classics written to date and must be considered by anyone conducting serious research on insurgency and counterinsurgency.

Dr. Bard O'Neill

To ensure this research encompasses all the major aspects of an insurgency, an additional insurgency expert heavily referenced throughout is Dr. Bard O'Neill. O'Neill is a professor of international affairs at the National War College, Washington, D.C. where he is the Director of Middle East Studies and Director of Studies of Insurgency and Revolution. A 1979 Senior Research Fellow at the National Defense University, O'Neill has served as a consultant to various high-ranking officials in the Departments of State (DoS) and Department of Defense (DoD) concerning Israel, Jordan, Egypt, Saudi Arabia, Iran, and other countries.

In his book, *Insurgency and Terrorism: From Revolution to Apocalypse,* O'Neill identifies the factors he contends that gave rise to historical insurgencies and compare and contrast these cases. O'Neill highlights the particularly violent situations that arose where societal divisions were cumulative and were combined with economic and political disparities. He states, ―Whether it was the Philippines in the early 1950s, Cuba in the late 1950s, Laos and Vietnam in the late 1950s and 1960s, or El Salvador, Guatemala, Nicaragua, and Peru in later years, the story was a familiar one: small ruling establishments supported by vested interests (e.g., landowners, the military, or religious leaders) controlled the lion's share of economic wealth and political power."[3] Since these are some of the social and economic conditions identified in Mexico, O'Neill's research will provide additional breadth and depth into some of the general aspects of insurgency and counterinsurgency addressed in FM 3-24. O'Neill's research into a wide range of current and historical insurgencies will allow this research to better frame the current situation within Mexico and assist this study by helping to identify and clarify some the common aspects of insurgency, especially in areas where FM 3-24 lacks sufficient detail.

Mexican Drug Cartels

To understand the world of narco-trafficking and production, two institutions will be referenced. The first institutional source is The Strategic Studies Institute (SSI) located at the U.S. Army War College, Carlisle Barracks, Pennsylvania. Composed of civilian research professors and uniformed military officers, the SSI focuses on, ―global, trans-regional, and functional issues, particularly to those dealing with Army Transformation," and creates partnerships with the global strategic community to engage with the, ―foremost thinkers in the field of security and military strategy."[4] These studies analyze the world of drug trafficking, the drug trade and drug cartel operations and their influence from a strategic security perspective and provide excellent analysis for comparing the elements and dynamics of the drug cartels and an insurgency.

The second institutional source is the Federation of American Scientists (FAS). The FAS is an independent, nonpartisan think tank and membership organization, dedicated to providing, ―rigorous objective, evidence-based analysis and practical policy recommendations on national and international security issues connected to applied science and technology."[5] FAS will provide this research insight into the Mexican drug trafficking situation with experts in political science and strategic security. The FAS

articles used in this research also provided insight into recommendations for defeating the

narco-insurgency within Mexico.

The third type of source is recently published periodicals and newspapers.

Newspapers will allow this research to analyze current gang and cartel actions using

intimidation and violence as a means for achieving their desired goals and objectives.

Newspapers will also provide insight into current government estimates of the situation

within Mexico and what initiatives are being implemented by the government there to

combat these issues.

Mexican Political History

Research on Mexican history will be referenced in order to thoroughly understand

the evolution of the drug cartels and the roots causes of the social and economic issues

that exist within Mexico today. Mexican history, as far back as Spanish rule, is replete

with all manners of insurgencies and revolutions that, at various times in the nation's

history, either successfully or unsuccessfully fought for control of Mexico.

America's First Battles 1776–1965, was complied by a group of historians, ―each

a nationally known specialist in a particular period of military history,‖[6] and edited by

Charles E. Heller and William A. Stofft, both of whom were employed at the Combat

Studies Institute (CSI) located at the U.S. Army Combined Arms Center (CAC), Fort

Leavenworth, Kansas. Heller and Stofft edited these historical writings into general

concepts and created a, ―scholarly examination of the way the U.S. Army has prepared

for, fought, and learned from its first battles.‖[7] This reference, first published in 1986

provides essential detail into the initial interactions between the U.S. and Mexico to include the political environment that surrounded the U.S. Mexican War. This political environment and detail is essential to the research because it provides insight to the roots of the current restrictions on military opinions available to the U.S. and its desire to support the Mexican government's fight against the drug cartels.

The Course of Mexican History, by Michael C. Meyer and William L. Sherman published in 1983, provides a general level of detail for researching historically significant events such as the Mexican Revolution of 1910, while providing commentary on the surrounding social, economic, and political situation in Mexico during this period. This reference was helpful in determining the origin of the Mexican drug cartels and offered great insights into the ever increasing gap between the social classes in Mexico. Meyer is a Professor of History at the University of Arizona, a former general editor of the Hispanic American Historical Review, and is a former president of PROFMEX, the Consortium of United States Research Programs for Mexico. Sherman is a professor of History at the University of Nebraska-Lincoln.

Mexican Politics: The Containment of Conflict, originally published by Martin C. Needler, a political scientist at the University of New Mexico, in 1996, provides this research details into the political and economic impacts of initiatives such as the North American Free Trade Agreement (NAFTA), and their impact on the population and how they further effected the separation between the social classes in Mexico. *Mexican Politics,* also contains vital information about the Haciendas system, the evolution of the Institutional Revolutionary Party (PRI), and facts relating to the historical social and economic situation leading up to the Mexican Revolution of 1910.

Mexico: Paradoxes of Stability and Changes, by Daniel Levy and Gabriel

Szekely, published in 1987 provides excellent background into the economic issues

concerning agricultural trade between the U.S. and Mexico and the evolution of an

underground, black market, created by government intervention, to distribute narcotics

and heavily taxed goods. Levy is an Associate Professor of Latin American Studies and

Educational Administration and Policy Studies at the State University of New York

(SUNY) at Albany; a faculty fellow at the Nelson A. Rockefeller Institute of

Government; and a research affiliate at Yale University. Szekely, is a professor at the

Center of International Studies, El Colegio de Mexico, and once the acting associate

director at the Center for U.S. Mexican Studies located at the University of California in

San Diego.

Mexico Under Siege: Popular Resistance to Presidential Despotism, by Donald

Hodges and Randy Gandy, published in 2002, provides an in-depth look at many of the

causes that fueled discontent in insurgent groups leading up to the Mexican Revolution of

1910 and is still influencing Mexican politics today. This book provides an outline of

historical insurgencies and allowed this research to compare today's situation in Mexico

to these historical cases. Hodges is a Professor of Philosophy and Affiliate Professor of

Political Science at Florida State University. Gandy studied philosophy, history, and

economics at the University of Heidelberg, Mexico and Texas and currently teaches

Sociology at the National University, in Mexico.

Popular Movements and Political Change in Mexico, a collection of works edited

by Joe Foweraker and Ann L. Craig, address the evolution of the Mexican political

institution. This reference was used to provide additional background information into the

Institutional Revolutionary Party (PRI), the one party system that ruled Mexico

throughout the 20th Century.

Chapter 3 will discuss the research method in which Mexican history,

counterinsurgency manuals, and current reports on the drug cartels will be used to outline

the elements that make-up the narco-insurgency the Mexican government is facing.

------

[1]Matthew A. Lauder, *Religion and Resistance: Examining the Role of Religion in Irregular Warfare* (Toronto: Defense R&D Canada, 2009), 4.

[2]Gian P. Gentile, ─Our coin doctrine removes the enemy from the essence of war," *Armed Forces Journal* (2006), http://www.armedforcesjournal.com/ 2008/01/3207722 (accessed 3 January 2001).

[3]Bard E. O'Neill, *Insurgency and Terrorism: From Revolution to Apocalypse*, 2nd ed. (Dullus: Potomac Books, 2005), 4.

[4]Strategic Studies Institute, ─About Us," http://www.strategicstudies institute.army.mil/ (accessed 3 January 2011).

[5]Federation of American Scientists, ─About FAS," http://www.fas.org/ (accessed 17 October 2010).

[6]Jack Bauer ─The Battles on the Rio Grande: Palo Alto and Resaca de la Palma, 8-9 May 1846," in *America's First Battles 1776- 1965*, edited by Charles E. Heller and William A. Stofft (Lawrence, KS: University Press of Kansas, 1986), ix.

[7]Ibid.

CHAPTER 3

RESEARCH METHODOLOGY

The Purpose of the Research

The purpose of this research is to determine if the operations, actions, and activities being conducted by the various Mexican drug cartels, with support from their network of street gangs and individuals from the lower class of Mexican society, qualifies as an insurgency as defined by a combination of the U.S. Army's Field Manual (FM) 3-24, *Counterinsurgency,* and other counterinsurgency references. This research will show that the cartels are waging a narco-insurgency using a combination of political and social influence to achieve its strategic goals of continuing to earn income from unlimited illegal economic profits. This research will show that the root causes and support for this insurgency are a result of long term inequalities between the social classes within Mexico. This will be done by examining historical events and long lasting social and economic issues within Mexico while framing the situation with the most current counterinsurgency doctrine. This research will also provide recommendations for the Mexican government to consider while combating this narco-insurgency and suggest possible support functions the U.S. can perform to aid Mexico in their fight.

The Organization of Chapter Three

Chapter 3 will consist of three parts. First, this chapter will discuss how the data was collected and the steps that were taken to avoid bias. Second, this chapter will discuss the research method used to answer the primary and secondary questions. Finally, this chapter will discuss the limitations placed on this research.

Data Collection

This qualitative research will be conducted in the form of a case study which involves creating a theoretical lens or framework to view a social, economic, or political environment or —ease." In this research the theoretical lens will be the irregular warfare style of insurgency. The case in this research consists of a combination of social and economic issues currently facing Mexico, the objectives of the various drug cartels and their narco-trafficking operations, and the complex network of street gangs that supports the drug cartels using violence and intimidation tactics.

In this study, research will primarily be conducted by literature review. To define the theoretical lens for insurgency a literature review of the U.S. Army's COIN manual, FM 3-24, *Counterinsurgency*, and the books, *Insurgency and Terrorism: From Revolution to Apocalypse,* by O'Neill and, *Counterinsurgency Warfare: Theory and Practice,* by Galula will be utilized. These three sources will provide a theoretical lens by defining the elements and dynamics of an insurgency. To understand the roots of the drugs cartels and to analyze the evolution of social and economic oppression throughout Mexican history, a literature review involving numerous Mexican political and historical documents will also be used. To understand the current situation involving the drug cartels and their effects on Mexico and the U.S., two primary resource organizations will be used; they are the SSI and the FAS. This research will also observe current events from newspapers, magazine articles, and websites to capture the most recent initiatives by the Mexican government in combating the insurgency threat and the latest acts of intimidation by the drug cartels. Finally, the researcher will make a summary and conclusion while providing possible counterinsurgency recommendations, based on the previously mentioned counterinsurgency references, for the government of Mexico and possible supporting actions for the U.S.

This research will adhere to two aspects of data collection to ensure validity; the use of multiple sources and the attempt to eliminate bias. Multiple sources of data will be used to provide a solid theoretical lens that encompasses all the characteristics of an insurgency to successfully create a thorough definition and complete outline of the elements and dynamics indicative of an insurgency. This research will also remain aware of and ensure that bias from the researcher's own personal experiences with counterinsurgency operations and from the authors of the various sources used in this research, is limited when interpreting facts and describing the social and economic issues within Mexico.

The Method

To analyze the situation within Mexico this qualitative research paper is a case study on drug cartels in Mexico. The case study method was chosen since this method is usually used to, ‑develop theories when partial or inadequate theories exist for certain populations and samples or existing theories do not adequately capture the complexity of the problem we are examining."[1] Specifically, this research will show that the situation in Mexico is an insurgency and warrants greater and more effective initiatives than can be offered by law enforcement agencies to quell the violence and to bring the situation under control. This research will delve deeper into the social and economic issues that drive the support for the drug cartels and the gang lifestyle which can inform future research into theories and solutions that are much more counterinsurgency focused, in addition to the current law enforcement efforts.

In order to solve the primary question of, ¬Are the drug cartels and their network of supporting street gangs an insurgency within Mexico?" this research divided the different elements into more specific secondary questions and research. To understand the situation in Mexico, this research began by analyzing Mexican history and the evolution of the drug cartels and gangs along with the social and economic issues that have plagued the country for decades.

Next, this research defined the term insurgency using a combination of historical and more recent insurgency and counterinsurgency experts. This provided an outline of all the elements, characteristics, and dynamics of an insurgency creating a lens in which to view the drug cartels, drug operations, the drug network, street gangs and current and historical social, economic, and political issues within Mexico. Using both Mexican history and the outline and definitions for all the elements and dynamics of an insurgency, this research was able to show what role the cartel leadership plays, how narco-trafficking finances operations, and how support of the population is involved in forming an insurgency.

Finally, with the help of counterinsurgency reference material, this research made recommendations for possible solutions to the narco-insurgency by first identifying the vulnerabilities of an insurgency and focusing government, military, and law enforcement efforts towards the vulnerabilities that seemed indicative of a narco-insurgency.

Limitations

As stated in his book, *Qualitative Inquiry and Research Design,* John W. Creswell notes that detail, ¬can only be established by talking directly with the people, going to their homes or places of work, and allowing them to tell the stories unencumbered by what we expect to find or what we have read in the literature."[2] The method for collecting data for this research will mainly be done by literature review and observing and monitoring internet sources. This separation from the people will inject a gap between what is reality and perceived reality.

---

[1]John W. Creswell, *Qualitative Inquiry and Research Design: Choosing Among Five Approaches,* 2d ed. (Thousand Oaks: Sage Publications, Inc., 2007), 40.

[2]Ibid.

CHAPTER 4

ANALYSIS

Introduction to Chapter Four

In chapter 4, this research will identify many of the common attributes associated with current and historical insurgencies and draw parallels to show that the current situation within Mexico is in fact an insurgency.

First, we will look back at historical Mexican revolutions and the evolution of Mexican politics throughout the 20th Century to understand the roots of the problems we see today. This history review will start with the U.S.–Mexican War to show the initial fragmentation of the Northern territories Mexico lost in battles with the U.S. This fragmenting of territory and loss of control by the central government of Mexico will continue as the Haciendas System is created and instilled into the Mexican political environment. The Haciendas System, which started during the Spanish reign over Mexico as small farms, became better known as a consolidation of large areas of land that were distributed among only a few wealthy families.

This consolidation of land resulted in creation of a shadow government amongst the wealthy land owners and represented the establishment of an oligarchy form of rule within Mexico. This oligarchy of wealthy Mexican families, who control the majority of the territory and industry in Mexico, will create such a separation of the classes within the Mexican society that corruption, low pay, and harsh working conditions will serve to unite the lower class of people and result in a revolution. This research will show that the same causes and ideology that fueled the groups of people who participated in the

Mexican Revolution of 1910, also serves as a base for and supports today's narco-insurgency in Mexico.

Second, while there has been much written in recent years on this topic, this research will further define the term insurgency. This will be done in two steps. First, this research will compare and contrast the many different definitions provided by multiple military counterinsurgency doctrines or doctrinal manuals along with the definitions espoused by some of the leading experts and thinkers within the field in the growing volumes of literature. The intent of this research will be to identify the key elements and typical dynamics that comprise an insurgency.

Second, using all the definitions, key elements, and typical dynamics of an insurgency provided by the leading experts and current military manuals on this subject, this research will analyze the situation today in Mexico to show that it is an insurgency, specifically an economic based narco-insurgency complete with an ideology, objectives, and an organization.

Mexican History

Introduction

The conditions that set in motion the Mexican Revolution of 1910 continued throughout the 20th Century and fueled the creation of the base foundation of and long lasting public support for the lucrative but illegal business know as narco-trafficking. In the early 1900s Mexico found itself in the midst of an industrial revolution. Plantation owners received faster and newer farming and milling equipment causing them to rapidly buy land to expand farming production. Adding to this industrial growth, the U.S. was investing in businesses and factories in Mexico. The president of Mexico during these times of change was, President Ciudad Porfirio Diaz, who was responsible for ushering in this new era of industrial and economic growth that was spreading across the country.

Prior to 1910, the economic growth in Mexico was at the expense of the lower classes who were being overworked, pushed off their land, and received little if any of the profits that the middle and upper classes were reaping. Entire families including the children, worked seven days a week, from morning until night, since child labor laws and labor unions were non-existent. The Mexican Revolution of 1910 was an attempt by the people to bring about a change to these poor conditions; however; post revolution historians agree that the conditions in Mexico deteriorated before improving.

After 1920, and millions of dead citizens as a result of the fight for control of Mexico, the ensuing decades saw the evolution of a political one party system which, like the government before and Haciendas system, continued to profit enormously from the low worker wages that began to attract international businesses to Mexico. This period saw the evolution of labor unions which promised change, however, corruption of union leadership continued to suppress the lower working class of Mexico. As the 20th Century came to a close, farmers throughout rural Mexico, who were out of business as a result of the industrialization of Mexico, discovered there was a high demand for drugs in the U.S. This demand for drugs, in turn, created a lucrative business proposition that could easily provide a fast and reliable means for the lower class to free themselves as well as their communities from decades of poverty giving rise to the creation of drug cartels. With their beginnings as small plantations, the Mexican drug cartels began with the creation of small organizations and networks to produce, manufacturer, smuggle into, and distribute narcotics across the U.S. As their profits grew, so did their organization and their power.

31

Many cartels throughout Mexico slowly became responsible for their entire communities as they could provide better pay and services to the people in areas of the country where the Mexico Government was either weak or non-existent.

The Separatist Traditions of Mexico

Adopting a system of government that reflected the same dynamics of the government installed by the Spanish explorers and settlers decades before, Mexican territories were usually self-governing and linked to the central government by an appointed official. However a more extreme fragmentation of Mexico caused by internal and external reasons began shortly after the country won its independence from Spain at the beginning of the 19th Century.

Before having an opportunity to strengthen the power of its central government, Mexico faced an external threat from the north, from the U.S. Newly formed, both the U.S. and Mexican governments were in their infancy. As states within the two countries were being formed and borders being delineated between the two it was the, prescience of the three Mexican states of Texas, New Mexico, and Alta California in the path of the inexorable westward drive of American settlement that brought the two countries to war."[1]

Until 1845 conflicts between the U.S. and Mexico had been settled diplomatically however, the annexation of Texas in the spring of that year, severed diplomatic ties,"[2] between the two countries. The annexation was quickly supported by military might with the U.S. sending a small force of army regulars, commanded by Brevet Brigadier General Zachary Taylor, to ensure that security along the newly drawn border was honored and enforced, and that the American settlers were protected against the threat of retribution from Mexico.

The U.S. continued to push westward into new territories, however, the U.S. Government decided to adopt a new strategy for acquiring land using diplomatic means as opposed to the military annexation using force which was the technique used to acquire Texas. This new strategy began when President Polk, realizing the Mexican government was bankrupt set about to, exact more than, ~~$~~5 million in outstanding American claims against Mexico,"[3] and instead of currency offered to Mexico that America would gladly accept the northern territories of New Mexico and California in exchange for payment. To broker the deal, President Polk sent John Slidell to Mexico City, however, the Mexican Government refused to entertain the offer. Repeated attempts to negotiate the deal were made, but diplomatic means were exhausted when the Mexican Army, ~~l~~aunched a drive to remove the Americans from the disputed area, which brought the Battles of Palo Alto and Resaca de la Palma,"[4]

The U.S. Government responded to the Mexican assault by launching, ~~an~~ amphibious assault into the heartland of central Mexico. That campaign, brilliantly conducted by Major General Winfield Scott, ultimately forced Mexican politicians to negotiate and gained for the U.S. the great swath of territory that stretched from Texas to the Pacific and from Oregon to Baja California."[5]

The Haciendas System

In the late 19th Century in Mexico, the majority of the population lived in the rural areas outside of the cities. The landscape was filled with small scale, family centric, farms called Haciendas. Many of those who worked and lived on these farms had inherited the land from their fathers and grandfathers before them who had also worked the land and used it to support their families. The owner of the haciendas, the hacendados, was the person responsible for the well being of his family and for overseeing the self-sufficiency of the farm. The hacendados, who owned larger farms, were responsible for all the profits of the estate and providing welfare not just for his family but for the families of his workers as well; however, at the time, very little farm production was used or available for profit. The hacendados sold some of their surplus production in local or a regional markets however, the emphasis was on, ―self-sufficiency."[6] This self-sufficiency amongst the larger, more powerful haciendas owners, established the basis of a patronage system within Mexico.

In the years leading up to Mexico's Industrial Revolution there was a rapid increase in the harvesting of natural resources throughout the country. To capitalize on these resources, the government of Mexico advertised and invited private companies such as the railroad, oil, and mineral industries, to survey and develop the land. In 1883 a new land law was enacted by the Mexican government that was designed for the, ―foreign colonization of rural Mexico, [and] authorized land companies to survey public lands for the purpose of subdivision and settlement."[7] In payment for their efforts, the companies were rewarded with one-third of the land that they surveyed. The other two-thirds of the land was offered up for auction to wealthy Mexican families or foreign companies to purchase.

Numerous issues began arising across Mexico when the poor, small scale farmers, or lower class, were forced to produce documentation that entitled them to the land their families lived on. Many farmers could not produce the required documentation and only

34

knew that the land had been farmed by their fathers and grandfathers and handed down through the generations. Those families who could produce documentation where usually told by government officials that the paperwork was incomplete, improperly signed and or notarized. ─Within five years after the land law became operative, land companies had obtained possession of over 68 million acres of rural land and by 1894 one-fifth of the total land mass of Mexico."[8] Once small scale farmers began to lose their land while the wealthy families began expanding and consolidating the haciendas.

Soon, wealthy hacendados owned thousands of smaller haciendas which resulted in single families owning large, state sized portions of Mexico often comprised of land totaling over one million acres in size. Thus the Haciendas system, as it is known today, was born. Just as the U.S.-Mexican War fractioned off large Northern sections of Mexican land from the control of the government, the Haciendas system further subdivided the remainder of the region. Control of the states within Mexico came to rest more in the hands of the families who owned the land to include all the economic and natural resources than the Mexican government was responsible for in the area but the haciendas controlled. The formation of these large estates resulted in the formation of an oligarchy in Mexico with the power structure of the country placed in the hands of only a few powerful men. The haciendas took on a new meaning once it transformed from a small farm to a large plantation, the haciendas in Mexico soon, ─formed the basic economic unit of the country and also had social and political functions."[9] For those towns that would not sale to the hacendados, the hacendados employed acts of intimidation or internal embargos aimed at starving the town of work and badly needed supplies to influence the town's decide in favor of the haciendas.

Hacendados and their family members formed an oligarchy government within Mexico by serving as, or influencing, all forms of governance for their region. If the Hacendados was not the ‑elected official," it was common that someone within the family was appointed as the head governmental official for the region. ‑This patronage amongst the rich to grant privileges or appoint a person to positions within the government is evident in the state of Chihuahua, whose governing body brought wealth and prestige to one extended family."[10] The state of Chihuahua was owned by Don Luis Terrazas who founded and controlled the state through the Terrazas-Creel clan. The wealth of the Terrazas family was not just in land ownership, ‑Don Luis also owned textile mills, granaries, railroads, telephone companies, candle factories, sugar mills, meat packing plants and several Chihuahua mines."[11] Enrique Creel, who married into the Terrazas family and became partners with his father-in-law Don Luis, served as the state's governor, just as Don Luis had done previously, and owned iron and steel mills, breweries, granaries, and a coal company.

The haciendas system created two issues for the Mexican government. First, it further subdivided and fractured the land and its people pulling them away from the control of the central government. Second, the hacendados created an oligarchy and or shadow government that controlled Mexican politics and influenced and implemented policy that further benefited the family's profits. This patronage within the government resulted in the majority of families throughout Mexico finding, ‑themselves in dying villages or subsisting as peones [rural farm workers] on the nation's haciendas [and] were worse off financially than their rural ancestors a century before."[12]

Labor Conditions Prior to the Revolution

Historians have shown that numerous causes ignited the Mexican Revolution in 1910. This section will focus on the conditions of the lower class workers in Mexico. Just after the turn of the century, the economic climate in Mexico, ―shunned the masses,‖ and the economic surplus, ―had been appropriated by the few.‖[13] In other words, there was a growing separation between the social classes within Mexico and the political environment that fueled the oppression of the lower working class.

The change that made the 1910 Revolution possible was, ―an increasing number of young, socially aware Mexicans,‖ that in the late 19th Century ―had begun to lay bare the social malaise of the old regimes.‖[14] As this new ideological view began to influence the masses within Mexico, political activists attempted to propose social change to the dictatorship or dictatorial style of government run by President Diaz. An example of this was the Liberal Plan in 1906 that called for, among many other issues, a nationwide eight-hour workday and six-day workweek, the prohibition of child labor, and the payment of all workers in legal tender. This peaceful process of change gained popularity across Mexico; however it had little influence over the government of Mexico.

The peaceful and diplomatic means to improve labor conditions would only last so long before workers across Mexico began to violently express their discontent with their social situation. Two examples of labor unrest and the Mexican government's willingness to protect foreign investment over the lives of its own citizens were, the Cananea Consolidated Copper Company incident and the killings at Rio Blanco Textile Mills.

The Cananea Consolidated Copper Company

The Cananea Consolidated Copper Company was owned by an American named Colonel (COL) William Greene. Mexican workers at the mine were upset because, ―Mexicans were paid less than their United States counterparts for performing the same jobs.‖[15] ―Qualified Mexican laborers were consigned to undesirable posts, while the technical and managerial positions were staffed entirely by U.S. personnel.‖[16] On 1 June 1906 the workers walked out on strike and began to consolidate around the mine‗s lumber yard, but were quickly stopped by guards who closed and locked the gates. The protestors were angered and attempted to break down the fence to gain access to the lumber yard. COL Greene and many of his American workers began to fear for their lives and requested assistance to quiet the riots from their political affiliates back in Arizona. Soon after the message was received in the U.S., two hundred plus, Arizona Rangers were illegally dispatched to Mexico, sneaking across the border in pairs to avoid creating an international incident, and consolidated at the mine.

Upon arrival of the Arizona Rangers, violence soon broke out with both American and Mexicans losing their lives that day. In the aftermath, numerous Mexican workers were hung in the streets of Cananea as a form of ―justice‖ for their opposition and actions during the strike and the ensuing skirmish. The Mexican government made no attempt to reprimand the offending company or the U.S. for their actions. This incident at Cananea demonstrated to the people that the oligarchy system of government in Mexico was willing to let its people die in order to protect foreign investment and continue the push for economic profits.

The Rio Blanco Textile Mills

At the Rio Blanco Textile Mills, Mexican workers approached the mills leadership concerning child labor within the mill. Workers were concerned because ―children of eight and nine years of age performed physically demanding work."[17] Their concerns were summarily dismissed on the morning of 6 January 1910 and soon after, ―the workers held a mass meeting and decided to strike the following day."[18] The strike was peaceful, however, when the families of the workers went to the market that day they were denied service by the local vendors. A verbal confrontation ensued between the worker's families and various shop owners causing the incident quickly deteriorated further into pushing and shoving. Soon local authorities began firing at the families which resulted in many of them lying dead in the street. When other family members came to retrieve the bodies of their loved ones, they too were shot and left for dead in the street. Much like the incident at Cananea, Mexican lives were sacrificed solely in the name of economic profits for the continued benefit of the wealthy families of Mexico.

The incidents at Cananea and Rio Blanco demonstrated to the people of Mexico that protecting foreign investment was the priority of their government. The government was willing to kill and or allow its own people to be killed in order to maintain an uninterrupted flow of economic profits and industrial growth. Today Mexico continues to use its ability to provide cheap labor as an advantage to attract foreign investment to the country. This advantage has spawned an economic imbalance throughout Mexico. The shift from an agricultural economy to that of an industrial economy means that stable, honest, and legitimate work can only be found in factories located around the country's major cities. This has resulted in the rural farm areas becoming even poorer and in some cases, ungoverned. These conditions not only fueled the insurgent groups that started the Mexican Revolution of 1910, but continue to fuel the narco-insurgency that the Mexican government faces today.

President Jose de la Cruz Porfirio Diaz Mori

President Porfirio Diaz became president of Mexico in 1876, when the country —was hopelessly backward. It had scarcely been touched by the scientific, technological, and industrial revolutions or the material conquests of the nineteenth century."[19] During President Diaz's regime, Mexico entered a modernization period that it had never seen before. Major breakthroughs in steam, water, and electric power, health and sanitation improvements, helped lead to the railroad boom, the revival of mining, and the spread of oil and other industrial enterprises across Mexico. Although improvements in industry and economics were sweeping across the country, the political environment was being controlled by a harsh dictator.

President Diaz consolidated his control and remained in power from 1876 to 1911 by way of, —a combination of adroit political maneuvering, threats, intimidation, and, whenever necessary, callous use of the federal army and the rurales."[20] These tactics of maintaining the peace through power within the prospering country were necessary since the modernization of Mexico was achieved at the expense of the lower working classes. With all the positive changes and improvement in Mexico, at the end of the day, —the plight of the urban laborer had changed little."[21]

The Revolution Begins

All across Mexico the people's voices were beginning to speak out against the Diaz regime however, these were individuals that Diaz could easily silence as they lacked leadership, organization, and active public support mostly out of fear of reprisal from the government. The peoples or worker's cause found a benefactor and leader in Francisco I. Madero. Madero was the son of a wealthy hacendados owner, was well educated, and had sympathy for the workers on his family's farm. Madero began an "anti-re-election" campaign against Diaz in June of 1910 which immediately led to many of Madero's supporters being targeted by the "Diaz run" police force. In an attempt to hide his supporters from the brutal Diaz regime, Madero began lying to officials about the whereabouts of some of his key political cadre resulting in, Madero himself being, "arrested for abetting a fugitive from justice.

In reality his only crime had been to dare to oppose Diaz in the 1910 presidential elections."[22] Madero finally realized that his efforts to, "unseat the dictator by constitutional means," had failed. It only resulted in violence being used against his supporters and that now his only option would be to, "call his fellow Mexicans to arms in the task of national redemption."[23]

Despite a period of prosperity for Mexico a combination of dissatisfied laborers, the increasing separation of the social classes, and the harsh dictatorship of President Diaz, began the Mexican Revolution of 1910. However, the revolution initial success of ousting the dictatorship, only ushered in a period of widespread violence and constant political change leaving millions of Mexicans dead.

During the next eighty six years, Mexicans saw little change in conditions for the lower class workers despite the Revolution and all the promise that it brought. Most historians would agree that the situation in Mexico rapidly declined during this period in the country's history into what is known as "That Age of Violence." The Revolution had promised change, however Mexican's only saw, "rapid changes in the presidential chair, the heated debates in Aguascalientes and Queretaro, and the rebounding phrases of the Constitution of 1917 surely had little immediate meaning to the Mexican masses."[24] Revolutionary leaders turned against each other and civil war broke out across the land resulting in the killing thousands of Mexicans.

Out of all this upheaval in Mexican politics a one party system evolved, coming into power with the creation of the Revolution Institutional Party (PRI). Experts agree that the Mexican Revolution of 1910, "almost completely destroyed Mexico's past and forged a new and somewhat different nation,"[25] however, corruption and greed were too deeply engrained into Mexican politics for even the Revolution to destroy. The PRI was, "the single, all-powerful mechanism of electoral activity, recruitment, and social control."[26]

As Mexico's economy began to recover and rapidly advance from the shambles the Revolution created, political elites within the PRI continued to gain power and wealth through manipulation of the party mechanisms. The one party system within Mexico had, "enshrined Mexican personal freedom of political opinion, while systematically repressing political organizations that operated outside the limits allowed by the PRI."[27] Just as it had ruled prior to the Revolution, the Haciendas system was now revitalized in

42

Mexico. This oligarchy of political elites continued to ensure the exploitation of the Mexican worker and controlled government policy for their own profits.

Throughout the 20th Century Mexican politicians at all levels ran on campaign slogans that promised changes in labor laws and better working conditions in all aspects of the Mexican economy. The reality is that once in office, the politicians rarely followed through with their promises and when they did, corruption within the middle class prevented any serious, long lasting changes. In Mexico's rapidly advancing economy, ―The very poor get left behind. Most of the working class runs hard to stay in the same place. The very wealthy do well, but no longer monopolize society's wealth; they must move over to make way for the major beneficiaries of development, the middle class."[28]

The middle class was made up of mostly workers, ―whose union membership or whose employment in modern factories provides them with above-average wages, fringe benefits, and employment security, along with office workers in the public and private sectors, and operators of small businesses."[29] As promising as that sounds only a small portion of the Mexican work force is unionized. Experts estimate that only between, ―20 percent and 25 percent of workers in urban areas,"[30] have union representation while rural workers have none. This is compounded by the fact that even though Mexico is known today for having relatively peaceful labor relations, these favorable conditions are purchased by, ―employers' payments to union leaders."[31] Today, corruption takes on other forms besides the acceptance of favors from employers, such as, ―the abuse of union funds for personal ends, and the extortion of payments from workers in return for influence in securing desirable jobs."[32]

The Transformation from Haciendas to Cartel

In the latter half of the 20th Century the haciendas took on a new dynamic. Those families who chose to profit in an illegal economy, usually consisted of producing, manufacturing, and distributing narcotics, and other criminal activities, where soon labeled ―cartel." As the Mexican cartels emerged in society, it was clear that the cartel was modeled after the ancient haciendas. This was evident in the fact that the cartels, as did the haciendas, focused on self-sufficiency and manufacturing products for profits. The difference is that the cartels focused more towards operations within the illegal underground economy of Mexico. That is not to say that the cartels in Mexico did not, or do not own legal businesses, however, their main source of revenue comes from the black-market of narco-trafficking and other illegal products and services. An example of this evolution from an legal economy to the profitable illegal black-market is evident in the story of hemp production within Mexico.

In Southeast Mexico, hemp was farmed for the creation of rope, matting, and other products since the early 1930's. Hemp was a stronger and faster renewable resource than wood especially when it came to making paper and other products such as rope. About the same timeframe that hemp farming was growing in Mexico, in the U.S., hemp production was outlawed by the Marijuana Tax Act of 1937. This act was a result of many different influences. First, lumber companies and other fiber companies were not able to compete in quantity or quality with the products that hemp farmers produced. Therefore, lumber companies petitioned through local representatives, to have farming of hemp banned in the U.S. Second, to support the agenda of the lumber companies, a campaign was launched in the American media that depicted the message that smoking hemp made people crazy.

The outlawing of hemp production in the U.S. correlates with the beginning of a long decline in hemp production in the Southeastern Mexico, ⁻with the slack in the peninsula's economy being made up to some extent by the growth of tourism and textile production."[33] Despite the fact that hemp production was on the decline and the original market for hemp was eliminated, a new market with new and increasing demands emerged. This demand was again coming from the U.S. and affected farmers in Southeastern Mexico who were asked to keep producing hemp. ⁻Mexicans have argued that U.S. tariffs on legitimate goods, like vegetables push Mexican farmers into a more lucrative agricultural activity-the cultivation of drugs."[34]

Historically, the northern cities in Mexico were the areas that many of the leaders in the Mexican Revolution resided. This area has always been a thriving area for crossing points into the U.S., trade, and tourism. In the recent decades, industry has been increasing in these areas. American companies were building new factories which use, ⁻U.S. components and operate under bond, returning the finished product to the United States."[35] Similar to the social and economic situation that was present in Mexico prior to the Revolution of 1910, American companies are attracted to Mexico for the cost saving benefit of low worker wages. This industrialization of Mexico created a shift that is attracted workers to the factories, leaving the rural areas even poorer. Having witnessed decades of consistently poor conditions and low pay in the factories many hard working lower social classes in Mexico were attracted to the better pay and stability that the gangs and cartels within Mexico offered.

In the U.S., the demand for drugs was relatively low throughout the 1940s with a rapid increase occurring in the 1960s and a continual, steady increase throughout the following decades. Initially, the high demand for drugs was met by narco-trafficking from throughout the world, however, by 1986, Mexico reportedly increased production to become, ―the primary producer and source of heroin and marijuana and surged into second place (behind Columbia) as a conduit for cocaine."[36] To the Mexican Cartels the trafficking of drugs is simply a business. American's wanted drugs and, for a price, the cartels could deliver the goods. Initially, in the minds of the cartel leadership, their view was the transporting of a crop that had been produced naturally in Mexico for decades could not be terribly illegal.

The view of many Mexican's was that the cartels business of trafficking narcotics was not any worse than the ongoing and rampant corruption in the government and industry that Mexico had experienced for decades. Additionally, the sole responsibility for the narcotics being smuggled in, sold, and distributed in the U.S. cannot be blamed just on the cartels in Mexico, but instead on the U.S. demand. ―One must look at the *demand* side of the equation; without U.S. demand Mexicans would not grow the supply. Millions of U.S. consumers are in fact all too eager to pay billions of dollars for their illicit pleasures. Moreover, U.S. drug pushers benefit from the trade."[37]

A major problem in attempting to stop the adverse affects the illegal drug market that the cartels are creating for both U.S. and Mexican governments, lies in the widespread and popular demand for the drugs. There is a total lack of public support to pre-empt the distribution of drugs due to the fact that, ―no society-wide Mexico-United States consensus would emerge as long as many people rely on drugs to provide their

46

jobs, illicit incomes, pleasures, or escapes."[38] As stated before, the cartels are simply business men who provide a need that supplies a specific demand. They evolved from an illicit business venture into an insurgency when they began using military force, tactics, and techniques to exercise or enforce control over specific territory and to defend their narcotic trade routes.

Increased Violence

As the 21st Century began, the demand for drugs was consistently rising. Narco-trafficking was illegal however, the drug cartels and gangs operating along the U.S.-Mexican border felt little pressure from authorities to stop their efforts to move narcotics into the U.S. and return to Mexico with money and guns. Security along the southwestern border of the U.S. and Mexico had little law enforcement presence, yet both governments were treating drug trafficking as a law enforcement issue. The U.S. has been waging a war on drugs since President Nixon was in office in the 1970s, and while government counter-drug units and operations and spread across the U.S., the flow of drugs remained consistent along the southeastern border.

It was not until the 1990s that external and internal factors pushed the cartels from operating under the guise of a simple business model into that of a full blown drug insurgency. First, the terrorist attacks in New York City in 2001 forced Washington to crack down on illegal crossings along the southeastern border restricting the access of Mexicans, attempting to find jobs and send payments back to their home communities, many of which are bereft of males between the ages of 18 and 45."[39] The U.S. has also become extremely proficient, with the development of new technology and better tactics, at stopping maritime and aerial drug trafficking. Shutting down two of the three avenues

47

to smuggle drugs into the U.S. the cartels are now forced to utilize land routes to move their product.

Second, the North American Free Trade Agreement (NAFTA), ~~and~~ recent economic woes have increased the number of unemployed."[40] As the number of unemployed Mexican workers rises in the rural areas of the country, the pool in which the cartels can recruit from steadily increases. As the Mexican population becomes increasingly desperate for work and financial stability, the idea of joining and supporting the drug cartels becomes more lucrative.

Third, is the election of Mexican President Felipe Calderon who has implemented an aggressive campaign to stop the cartel's activities during his administration, and continues to apply military and law enforcement pressure on the cartels along the southern side of the border. Restricting the flow of illegal crossings along the southwestern border created both a positive and negative affects for the cartels. The positive affect for the cartels is an increase in recruiting, since a large percentage of those workers who are desperately seeking employment in the U.S. can no longer cross the border, will finally resort to supporting the drug insurgency to obtain pay and stability. The negative affect is that, with less access to the U.S., the cartel's must take additional measures to meet the U.S. growing demand for drugs. Cartels have resorted to using a combination of activities to offset reduced access ranging from increasing the volume of flow to account for product that is seized at the border, to employing new techniques to transport the product, and finally, resorting to the use of extreme violence against law enforcement agents if threatened with apprehension.

All three of these events, increased border patrols, NAFTA, and the aggressive actions of the newly elected President Calderon have increased the national focus on the issue of border security and operations of the drug cartels. The result of the increase in pressure and attempts to restrict the cartels freedom of movement has resulted in the cartels increasing their level of violence, major territorial disputes, and, in some cases separate cartels have turned their focus from fighting each other to combining their forces to secure and maintain their freedom of movement to sell their product.

The Definition of Insurgency

To show that the situation in Mexico is an insurgency, one must first understand the definition of insurgency. This research will first analyze the definition of insurgency as stated in current U.S. Joint and Army doctrine along with the definitions espoused by nationally renowned insurgency and counterinsurgency experts in the field, Dr. Bard O'Neill and David Galula. This analysis will provide a comparison and contrast of these definitions, ultimately combining them in an attempt to develop a better, more inclusive definition of the term insurgency, one that captures all the main points from each of these sources. Once we have an ―all encompassing" definition, this research will use this definition as lens to demonstrate that the Mexican government is faced with a serious narco-insurgency within their borders that, if left uncontained, could eventually grow and spread across the border resulting in the same type insurgency within the U.S.

First, we must consider the definition of the term insurgency as stated in current U.S. Joint doctrine, specifically Joint Publication 1-02, *Department of Defense Dictionary of Military and Associated Terms*. It states an insurgency is, ―an organized

49

movement aimed at the overthrow of a constituted government through the use of subversion and armed conflict."[41]

Second, the newly published, U.S. Army Field Manuel (FM) 3-24, *Counterinsurgency,* dated December 2006, defines an insurgency as, ―an organized, protracted politico-military struggle designed to weaken the control and legitimacy of an established government, occupying power, or other political authority while increasing insurgent control."[42]

Third, Bard O'Neill, in his book, *Insurgency and Terrorism: From Revolution to Apocalypse* defines an insurgency as, ―as a struggle between a non-ruling group and the ruling authorities in which the non-ruling group consciously uses political resources (e.g. organizational expertise, propaganda, and demonstrations) and violence to destroy, reformulate, or sustain the basis of legitimacy of one or more aspects of politics."[43]

Fourth, David Galula, in his book, *Counterinsurgency Warfare: Theory and Practice,* describes the violent conflict between insurgent and counterinsurgent as the, ―the action of the insurgent aiming to seize power-or at splitting off from the existing country . . . and from the reaction of the counterinsurgent aiming to keep his power."[44] It is important to note the aspect of ―splitting off from the existing country," because this helps define the scale of an insurgency. There is false perception that a movement can only be considered an insurgency if it has national level interests. National level might be the strategic long term goals for an insurgency, as we will discuss later, however to earn the title of ―insurgency," the movement can contain limited goals such as delegitimizing a local or state government. This dimension added by Galula suggests that an insurgency, by definition, can begin as small as a gang operating within a small town. Galula's

50

definition of an insurgency also adds the dimension of time as he states, ─An insurgency is a protracted struggle conducted methodically, step by step, in order to attain specific intermediate objectives leading finally to the overthrow of the existing order."[45] This aspect of time is important because it means that a movement can be deemed an insurgency in its infant stages, and does not require total success or failure in its culminating phases to earn the title of being an insurgency.

There are two common themes that run throughout each of these definitions. The first is, an insurgent seizes power with violence or the threat of violence. The second theme, which is not readily apparent, is the existence of oppression. An organization must be oppressed and desire change in order to be considered an insurgent. This is important because an organization that is not, or cannot prove they are oppressed, and uses violence to create fear for political change and influence, can be seen and defined as a terrorist.

Based on a combination of the definitions presented and after careful consideration from this point forward, this research will define an insurgency as:

> An organization that possess the capability to use violence and the other necessary resources to wage a protracted struggle whose strategic objective is focused on delegitimizing the control of an established government in attempts to split away from and or overthrow the ruling party.

In the following pages, this research will delve deeper into many of the characteristics of an insurgency previously mentioned and relate those to the current situation in Mexico. This research will show how the drug-trafficking cartels within Mexico have become a well financed narco-insurgency. These conclusions will be outlined by showing that the social condition of historical oppression of the Mexican lower class, combined with the capabilities and objectives of the cartels, to in essence form a narco-insurgency; that this Mexican narco-insurgency is complete meaning it

51

contains operational objectives focused on delegitimizing the government of Mexico in an effort to control the terrain or territory necessary to achieve their strategic objectives of continued economic gains through their network of worldwide narco-trafficking.

The Dynamics of Insurgency

This section is dedicated analyzing the dynamics and individual elements of an insurgency as defined by FM 3-24, *Counterinsurgency,* and Dr. Bard O'Neill's book, *Insurgency and Terrorism: From Revolution to Apocalypse.* As this research describes the different aspects of an insurgency, parallels will be drawn to the narco-insurgency in Mexico. He explains that the dynamics of an insurgency are characterized as:

1. Types of Insurgencies

2. The Criminal Element

3. Ideology and Objectives

4. The Organization, Elements, and Network

5. External Support

Introduction to the Dynamics of Insurgency

To better understand the dynamics of an insurgency one must first understand that each insurgency is unique. That is not to say that many historical and current insurgencies do not have common causes or attributes, they do, but even a single insurgency can be comprised of many different individuals who bring their own particular causes, ideologies, and objectives to the organization.

To categorize an insurgency means to identify its main cause. A cause is, "a principle or movement militantly defended or supported."[46] In order to gain support

52

insurgent leaders find a deep rooted and emotional cause that will identify with a large portion or segment of the population. The more people that can identify with, the cause, the greater the support and better the recruitment will be for the insurgency resulting in more forces, increased influence and reach.

The ideology of an insurgency consists of several parts to include main cause, additional supporting ideals, and general grievances that the population, identifies with along with potential solutions to help resolve or mediate these injustices against society. The ideology is then expressed through the insurgent's narrative which is their story of how these injustices were imposed upon society and how the cause was formed. The insurgent narrative is better understood as, ―an organizational scheme expressed in story form.‖[47]

The organization and its leadership begins to develop tactical, operational, and strategic level objectives based on the ideologies recommended solution(s) to the society's problem. Very similar to the type objectives found in conduct of conventional warfare, in an insurgency the strategic objective, ―is the insurgents end state.‖[48] Operational objectives are, ―those that insurgents pursue to destroy government legitimacy,‖[49] and build on other operational objectives to achieve the strategic objective. Tactical objectives can be summarized as what people read about in the paper; they are the, ―immediate aims of insurgent acts.‖[50] Just as operational objectives build to strategic end states, tactical objectives build to achieve operational objectives.

What makes the objectives of an insurgency unique from other forms of conflict though is the fact that the objectives in an insurgency are mostly psychological in nature as opposed to being based on physical terrain. If support of the population is characteristically one of the main tenets of an insurgency, then the objectives must change or influence the way the population thinks. For example, a conventional military force may seize a police station in order to establish an operational base from which they can assert additional control mechanisms over behavior attitudes and or movement of the population. An insurgency can gain support by simply bombing the police station in order to delegitimize the government in the eyes of the people. The table provided below will serve as a quick reference and overview outlining the dynamics of the insurgency and how that dynamic appears within the narco-insurgency.

Table 1. Dynamics of Insurgency			
Insurgency (FM 3-24)	Narco-Insurgency		
Leadership	√	√	Cartel, Street gangs, Prison Gangs
Crime	√	√	Producing, Manufacturing, and Distributing Narcotics
Objectives	√	√	Strategic: Economic Gains Operational: Geographic and political freedom of movement throughout central American and the U.S. Tactical: Legitimacy, Bribes, and Intimidation
Ideology and Narrative	√	√	The ideology speaks to the individual Mexican oppressed by government corruption, low pay, and harsh working conditions who wish to improve his or her social and economic status by joining a street gang and or actively and or passively supporting the drug trade.
External Support and Sanctuaries	√	√	External support is provided by the massive network of street gangs who distribute narcotics in the U.S. and in return deliver profits and or fire arms to the cartels in Mexico. Sanctuaries are found in small towns, dilapidated sections of major cities, and rural areas throughout Mexico where the people provide drug trafficking gangs and members of the cartel protection against other gangs and or the government.

Source: Created by author.

Types of Insurgency's and Their Causes

Insurgency's come in many different shapes and sizes. The nature of insurgency warfare has evolved throughout history to meet the needs of the people. FM 3-24 states that, ―Each insurgency is unique, although there are often similarities among them. In all cases, insurgents aim to force political change; any military action is secondary and subordinate, a means to an end.‖[51] Galula noted that an insurgency is usually defined by the problem or set of problems the leadership of the insurgency or people involved wish to solve. He goes on to say that, ―In other words, where there is no problem, there is no cause.‖[52] The cause and overall insurgency can be a variation or combination of political, economical, racial, and or social problems. The cause can even be artificial, according to Galula, just as long as there is a cause and it, ―has a chance to be accepted as fact.‖[53]

O'Neill agrees with the idea, and Galula's assertion, that a single insurgency can be comprised of numerous and evolving causes. In his book, O'Neill describes the following examples of insurgencies and their unique ideologies:

Anarchist: Highly diffuse and individualistic, their members believe that since all authority patterns are unnecessary and illegitimate, political systems should be destroyed but not replaced.

Egalitarian: Seeks to impose a new social system based on the ultimate value of distributional equality and centrally controlled structures designed to mobilize the people and radically transform the social structure within an existing political community.

Traditionalist: Seeks to restore a political system from the recent or distant past. Seek to establish political structures characterized by limited or guided participation and low autonomy, with political power in the clerical elites.

Apocalyptic-Utopian: A fringe insurgent grouping that merits brief attention includes religious cults with political aims, some of which transcend the confines of the nation-state. Essentially, they envisage establishing a world order-in some cases, involving divine intervention-as the result of an apocalypse precipitated by their acts of terrorism.

Pluralist: Aims to establish a system that emphasizes the values of individual freedom, liberty, and compromise and in which political structures are differentiated and autonomous.

Secessionist: Seeks to withdraw from the political community of which they are formally a part. (eg. confederate states)

Reformist: Targets policies that determine distribution of the economic, psychological, and political benefits that society has to offer. Those who have carried out acts of violence to effect policy changes related to abortion, animal rights, and the environment are among the most specific.

Preservationist: Differs from insurgents in all other categories in that they carry out illegal acts of violence against non-ruling groups and authorities that are trying to effect change.

Commercialist: Their main aim appears to be nothing more than the acquisition of material resources through seizure and control of political power. They consider political legitimacy to be relatively unimportant. Coercive power is what counts.[54]

This list is included to demonstrate the fact that insurgencies can have a wide spectrum of causes and ideologies. Although narco-insurgency is the term that is being used in this research to label the insurgency in Mexico, according to O'Neill's descriptions, the Mexican drug cartels most closely resemble a commercialist insurgency whose aims are to acquire material resources (narcotics) and profit from their sale, through the seizure and control of political power. However, commercialist only describes a portion of the narco-insurgency in Mexico which is much more complex and comprehensive being made up of a spectrum of individual social and economic causes most outwardly represented by the gang lifestyle.

The majority of political, military, and public officials have a perception that a movement can only be labeled an insurgency if it plans to overthrow a national level government. This perception and mindset is incorrect and is preventing both the U.S. and Mexican governments from seeing the enormity of the Mexican narco-insurgency and the threat it poses. The narco-insurgency is dangerous because it does not require a large, national level seizure of political power, but instead, only the slow infiltration of the local, state, and national level governments, whose insurgent members form a shadow government capable of influencing and controlling the political environment within the country. The narco-insurgency's political organization is seeming transparent, operating mostly unnoticeable, since its members are made up of corrupt government and or military officials. This, makes it hard to weaken the insurgent's political influence since it is well hidden from the counterinsurgency.

The Problem in Mexico

For the majority of the Mexican people, economic and social issues are at the root of their problems stemming all the way back to the Mexican Industrial Revolution and the events leading up to the Revolution of 1910. Galula defines economic oppression as, ―the low price of agricultural products in relation to industrial products in relation to industrial goods, or the low price of raw material in relation to finished products,"[55] Galula's definition is timeless and represents only a part of the issues plaguing Mexican society today. These economic problems are only compounded by the social issues that exist within Mexico. Social oppression is described by Galula as, ―when one class is exploited by another or denied any possibility of improving its lot."[56] When looking back at the history of Mexico, one of the main systemic problems throughout times past is Mexico's rural areas have traditionally had a low cost of living which influences wage earnings and equates to most Mexican's habitually being paid less for their services and labor than they contribute to legal businesses. This historically low pay amongst the majority of the population has prevented the working class from improving their social standing and quality of life.

Today, the Mexican economy is almost solely based on the backs of the lower working class providing cheap labor. Cheap labor is an advantage for the government as it continues to attract foreign investment and business however, it has created a shift in the economic landscape within Mexico. The standard of living amongst the rural farm areas has become poorer and essentially ungoverned with the governments focus being concentrated mainly on the industrial areas. The drug cartels have exploited these conditions, taking advantage of the opportunity it offers by giving the people a way to solve their economic and social problems while advancing the cartel's own monetary and political goals. The leadership of the cartels has identified how to combine these deep rooted social causes to gain the support of the people (popular support) to further their own agenda and cause. As demonstrated during the Revolution of 1910, the people of

Mexico are prepared to take action to advance these causes and seek some kind of means to improve their standard of living.

Just as Galula identified decades ago, ―The insurgent is not restricted to the choice of a single cause . . . he has much to gain by selecting an assortment of causes especially tailored for the various groups in the society that he is seeking to attract."[57] The fact that the cartels prey on the peoples egalitarian type values to recruit from the lower classes with the promise of increased social status and improved standard of living is how the cartel leadership is gaining momentum and popular support. Recent events in Mexico have proven that the drug cartels are also prepared to violently advance and defend their economic cause on a much larger scale than just relying on normal street crime. Applying the definition of insurgency as determined by this research, the drug cartels within Mexico are using political legitimacy to fulfill the necessary resources needed to achieve their end state of economic prosperity. The overwhelming issue that the Mexican government faces today is that these two causes, the cartel's combined with the people's cause, have united to form one of the most well funded insurgencies in history, with an ideology that touches all classes of society and identifies with populations throughout Mexico.

The Criminal Element and External Support

It is important to discuss the criminal element of insurgency before trying to understand the ideology and objectives of the narco-insurgency in Mexico. Funding for an insurgency is a very critical aspect and, ―greatly influences an insurgency's character and vulnerabilities."[58] One must understand that since an insurgency itself is illegal within the country it operates, funding for the insurgency most likely cannot be obtained through legal and or ethical channels. In order to purchase weapons, conduct propaganda, offer bribes, and sustain other requirements, insurgents must resort to either taxing the people or are forced to enter into relationships, ―with organized crime or into criminal activity themselves."[59] Historically, insurgents have found that, ―kidnapping, extortion, bank robbery, and drug trafficking-for favorite insurgent activities-are very lucrative."[60] External support also plays a key role in supplying an insurgency with the logistics needed to maintain its organization's capabilities. External support traditionally comes in the form of finances, weapons, safe heavens and recruitment. But what happens when the political objectives take a back seat to the more lucrative criminal activities? This is the essence of the narco-insurgency.

Today, Mexican officials face an insurgency whose core organization is solely focused on profits gained from criminal activity. The narco-insurgency's external support comes in the form of profits from sale of narcotics in the U.S. and American made weapons. The American public and gun manufacturers in the U.S. inadvertently and unknowingly provide the financial support and weapons to fuel the narco-insurgency in Mexico. Internally, Mexico has become a safe haven providing the freedom of movement needed for the cartels to operate.

Two historical examples of criminally based insurgencies are the Fuerzas Armadas Revolutionaries de Colombia (FARC) and the Maoist Communist Party of Nepal. Initially the FARC was an organization seeking political and social change for the rural poor against Colombia's wealthier classes. The FARC became solely focused on criminal activities such as drug trafficking and kidnapping once they realized that, ―profits from single kidnappings often total millions of U.S. dollars."[61]

The Maoist insurgency resorted to using forms of, "revolutionary taxation," such as extortion and kidnapping,"[62] when taxing the mass population base produce inferior results. These two organizations, the FARC and the Maoist insurgency, discovered that the political power they were striving to achieve did not begin to compare to the amount of financial power and huge monetary gain that organized crime could provide in support of their cause. These types of insurgencies are difficult to distinguish since their political goals are part of the means they use to gain access to other more lucrative criminal activities. In essences, this is exactly what is happening within Mexico.

The Ideology

The drug cartels seek to achieve enormous monetary gains through the continued production, transportation, and distribution of narcotics and other illegal non-narcotic activities. Insurgent groups within Mexico, finanaced by the cartels, "exercise violence to advertise their cause, radicalize the population, and move slowly but surely toward the achievement of their ideological and self-enriched dreams."[63]

These monetary gains acquired through narco-trafficking, are helping to solve many of the economic and social problems and disparities that have plagued Mexico for centuries. The cartels within Mexico form the leadership of these insurgent groups and have accrued a lot of popular support, "primarily as a response to historical sociopolitical factors. Mean while the Mexican political structure has not developed effective programs and policies to remedy the societal ills that are now generating recruits and popular support for all these _revolutionary' movements."[64]

Supporters of the cartels, through passive and active participation, indentify with the cause because as individual's, they believe that working for the cartels can improve their own socio economic status and overall quality of life. To rationalize and persuade the population to support its illegal activities, the cartel leadership, through the use of its political cadre, spreads propaganda comparing the mass government corruption of industry and the labor unions to the stability and cohesion found within the world of narco-trafficking.

The Objectives

The cartel leadership has identified that in order to maintain the cause for economic profit; two strategic objectives must be accomplished. First, the organization must achieve and maintain the capability to produce, transport, and deliver narcotics to the U.S. Second, the organization must prevent outside groups, rival cartels; and government agencies from interrupting their ability to conduct business.

The Strategic Objective

The drug cartels are comprised of businessmen who found an extremely lucrative supply and demand model trafficking drugs between the U.S. and Mexico. Their strategic goal and ultimate end-state is to continue to gain huge profits from their ability to freely move and distribute narcotics in the U.S. and to other countries around the world.

The Mexican and U.S. governments, as well as other governments worldwide affected by the flow of drugs from Mexico, are facing an economic insurgency that has possesses an ideology, objectives, and organization akin to that of a profit focused, fortune 500 company. As one journalist noted, —Mexican drug cartels generate more revenue than at least 40 percent of Fortune 500 companies, and the U.S. government's highest estimate of cartel revenue tops that of Merck, Deere, and Halliburton."[65]

The Operational and Tactical Objectives

In order to achieve their strategic goals and end state, the cartel leadership has established operational level objectives that focus on increasing their political influence and defending their territory with well financed militias. These objectives, coupled with their causes, are why the narco-insurgency of today is different from those of the past or what we think of as, traditional insurgencies. The difference between today's narco-insurgencies and insurgencies of the past is that the narco-insurgencies strive for political power as a means in order to enable the organization to achieve goals of huge economic profits and provides other advantages such as protection from rival cartels and government reprisals. Cartels sponsor public officials, representing the political cadre's arm of the insurgency, through infiltration or bribery or both, who on the surface fight and strive for economic and social change for the masses, but internally remain loyal to the cartels with the true intent of allowing them to continue their business ventures unabated.

To defend their territory, which includes safe heavens, lines of communication (LOC) and the flow of logistics into and out of the U.S., each cartel must maintain the public perception or persona of being a legitimate organization. The most common way to do this is to focus on operational and tactical objectives that directly delegitimize the government. The operational objectives of increasing political power and controlling more territory are two of the main reasons why the situation within Mexico has exhausted the resources of local law enforcement agencies resulting in a national level, cartel led, narco-insurgency.

For example, the tactical objectives that consist of using or employing persuasive and intimidating actions to sway the population and government officials during election periods have had, pernicious effects on democracy and tend to erode the will and ability of the state to carry out its legitimizing functions."[66] The ultimate threat the cartels pose is, (1) state failure, or (2) the violet imposition of a radical socioeconomic-political restructuring of the state and its governance in accordance with criminal values."[67] An example of the application of tactical objectives that achieve strategic effect is the cartels use and control of the media. Throughout the evolution of insurgency, media censorship has been a key technique in assisting insurgent groups to influence, control and shape the public's opinion, and exciting their support for the insurgency's cause. These lessons are not lost on the Mexican cartels. Despite the fact that the Mexican media is free from state censorship, journalist, academicians, and folk musicians who make their anti-narco-gang opinion know too publicly are systematically assassinated."[68]

Not all tactical and operational objectives of the cartels involve violence. Cartels also provide public support in order to peacefully legitimize and gain support for their cause, further de-legitimizing the government. Cartel leadership has been known to throw parades and festivals in towns within their safe havens. Historically, during the holidays, various cartel patrons throughout Mexico have donated massive amounts of toys and holiday materials to their communities. Additionally, in some areas, essential services have been installed or improved by the cartels as rewards for the people's active and passive support for the narco-trafficking industry and activities in the area.

In the absence of a strong state, criminal groups can provide public goods that would otherwise be lacking, and serve not just as a target of the state, but as

64

competition."[69] An example of this in today's Mexico is the cartel of La Familia who, "trumpets such social works as rebuilding schools, contributing to churches, and extending credits to farmers and businesses."[70]

The Organization

In order for a group of disgruntled citizens or a street gang of drug dealers to become an insurgency, the existence of some form of organization must be present. The organization symbolizes that the population is strong in their cause, their ideology, and are prepared to take the necessary steps to remedy those injustices. When evidence of these complex organizations, "commonly referred to as parallel hierarchies or shadow governments in the literature on insurgencies,"[71] appear, it is evident that the organization is poised to take action.

In Mexico today, the drug cartels and supporting street gangs make-up an extremely vast, complex, and fluid organization and network, that is fighting to achieve the objectives of an economic focused narco-insurgency. Mexican law enforcement and military forces are fighting against a shadow government formed by the drug cartels that encompasses all the elements necessary to be labeled a "narco-administration" who, "generates employment (in growing and processing drugs), keeps order (repressing rival cartels), performs civic functions (repairing churches), collects taxes (extorting businessmen), and screens newcomers to municipality (employing lookouts)."[72] These characteristics found in today's narco-insurgency are common throughout the evolution and history of insurgency warfare.

The distinguishing factor of a narco-insurgency's organization is the separate branch or arm of the insurgency whose sole focus is on the sale of narcotics. It is only

65

fitting that since the narco-insurgency in Mexico is an economic based insurgency, the cartels have also formed an organization that resembles the manufacturing and distribution chain of a major manufacturing company. To achieve their economic goals, the cartel employs, a host of ~~chief~~ executive officers and boards of directors, councils, system of internal justice, lawyers, accountants, public affairs officers, negotiators, and franchised project managers."[73] Many would agree that an organization who sells narcotics for profit is simply a law enforcement issue however, the cartels earn their narco-insurgency title based on their employment of, ~~a~~ security division, though somewhat more ruthless than one of a bona fide Fortune 500 corporation."[74] The security division is another element that clearly sets the narco-insurgency apart from other illegal and or criminal organizations and distinguishes it from the simple, low level narco-traffickers of the past particularly with its increase in scope and lethality.

Elements of an Insurgency

In this section we will analyze the elements that make up an insurgent organization. This research will first look at the general organization and elements that have become common elements in insurgencies as defined by FM 3-24, O'Neill, and Galula. We will then look at the drug cartels and show how they represent these elements within the insurgent organization. As outlined in FM 3-24, an insurgent organization normally consists of five elements. The table below outlines these five elements and how each one is represented within the Mexican narco-insurgency.

Table 2.			Elements of Insurgency
Insurgency (FM 3-24)			Narco-Insurgency
Movement Leaders	√	√	Cartel and Street Gang leadership
Combatants	√	√	Paramilitary forces, Enforcer Gangs, and Mercenary Groups
Political Cadre	√	√	Corrupt government, military, and law enforcement officials (Shadow Government)
Auxiliaries	√	√	Narcotics Producers, Manufacturers, Traffickers, Smugglers, and Distributers Look outs
Mass Base	√	√	The population that provides active or passive support for drug trafficking. This is the target population for recruitment by street gangs.

Source: Created by author.

The Movement Leader

The movement leader is the planner who generates the movement's ideas and provides direction through, ―force of personality, the power of the revolutionary ideas, and personal charisma."[75] The leadership of an insurgency is also responsible for the effectiveness of the organization and its personnel. O'Neill states that effective use of the people will, ―depend of the skill or insurgent leaders in identifying, integrating, and coordinating the different tasks and roles essential for success in combat operations, training, logistics, communications, transportation, and the medical, financial, informational, diplomatic, and supervisory areas."[76]

In the Mexican narco-insurgency, the insurgent leadership is represented by the top tiers of personnel in each of the cartels. For example; in the drug cartel, La Familia, ―who dominates narcotics sales in the lion's share of Michoacán's 113 municipalities,"[77] the leadership consists of four individuals ―El Chayo" Moreno Gonzalez, ―El Chango" Mendez Vargas, Enrique ―La Chiva" Plancarte Solis and Servando ―La Tuta" Gomez

67

Martinez. These men divide the responsibility of the drug trade by separating the territory between them. ‒El Chayo and El Chango are considered respectively the ‗brawn‘ and the ‗brains‘ of the syndicate, each has a responsibility for approximately half of Michoacán."[78] Solis, who reports to El Chayo, ‒has responsibility for coordinating drug sales to the United States."[79] Gomez Martinez, ‒serves as the syndicate‘s chief spokesman."[80]

The Combatants

The combatants are the foot soldiers who provide security and do the actual fighting for the movement. Based on the description provided by FM 3-24, combatants are sometimes mistaken for the movement itself, however, combatants, ‒exist only to support the insurgency‘s broader political agenda and maintain local control . . . they also protect training camps and networks that facilitate the flow of money, instructions, and foreign and local fighters."[81] In Mexico today, combatants are made up of three different levels of what could be considered, ‒privatized violence." In his article, *A "New" Dynamic in the Western Hemisphere Security Environment: The Mexican Zetas and other private armies,* Max Manwaring examines, ‒Transnational Criminal Organizations (TCOs) (cartels and mafia); small private military organizations such as the Zetas enforcer gangs (the Aztecas, Negros, and Polones); mercenary groups (the Central American Maras, Guatemalan Kaibiles, and paramilitary triggermen [gatilleros]); and other small paramilitary or vigilante organizations."[82]

In this research will we focus on the Zetas, a security organization made up of former members of the Mexican Army‘s elite Airborne Special Forces Group (GAFES). The Zetas defected in the late 1990s to support the Gulf Cartel and are considered, ‒to be the group most likely to be able to achieve their objectives . . . Zeta organization and planning has been outstanding, and the shock value of the Zeta operations has been unequaled."[83] Due to the Zetas effectiveness and lethality they pose the largest threat to the Mexican military and law enforcement. The Zetas provide the cartels with a capability for extreme violence, enough that the cartels can threaten the Mexican government as a legitimate insurgency.

The Zetas and other combatant organizations like them, create and consolidate semiautonomous enclaves (criminal free states) that develop into quasi states-and what the Mexican government calls Zones of Impunity'."[84] These organizations allow the leadership of the various cartels to develop quasi-state political entities where they, promulgate their own rule of law, negotiate alliances with traditional state and non-state actors, and conduct an insurgency-type war against various state and non-state adversaries."[85]

The Political Cadre

The political cadre forms the core of the insurgent movement and concentrates on achieving the movement's objectives, which in most cases, is winning the support of the people. The cadre, assess grievances in local areas and carries out activities to satisfy them."[86] As the scope and scale of an insurgency grows the responsibilities and reach of the cadre increases. Their influence can begin locally and increase to state and national level by, destroying the state bureaucracy and preventing national reconstruction after a conflict (to sow disorder and sever legitimate links with the people),"[87]

The role of the cadre varies based on the type organization of the insurgency adopts. Historically there have been three types of organizational structure's; First,

69

political leaders (cadre) are in charge and coordinate the efforts of the military wing; Second, separate political and military organizations strive to achieve the goals of the insurgency but have no coordination between the two; Third, the military is the lead organization. In this case, no political party is needed and leaders usually remain underground and out of the public spot light. What sets the narco-insurgency apart from other historical insurgencies is the fact that political influence is only an operational level objective to achieve as part of a higher strategic goal, thus leaving the leadership of the insurgency to the ―military like‖ hierarchy inherently a part of the cartels structure.

In the Mexican narco-insurgency the political goals are to establish territorial control so the cartels have the freedom of movement to transport their product throughout Mexico and the U.S. with the intentions of eventually expand their existing political and economic control. This means that the political cadre within a narco-insurgency is not necessarily a part of the leadership of the insurgency but does support the ideals of the organization. The combination of the two main causes, which are profits from narcotics trafficking for the cartels and social improvements for the working class in Mexico, the political cadre of this narco-insurgency has the ability to represent the moral objectives of the population's social cause while benefitting from lucrative finances gained through narcotics trafficking.

The cadre of these organizations establish control over the population through the use of two methods; shadow governments (parallel hierarchies) and infiltration. A key to establishing freedom of movement throughout an area is the recruitment of local officials. Recruitment is done with passive and active bribes. Passive bribes are when individuals are offered money to assist and or ignore drug operations within their area. Active bribes are when individuals are given money and instructed to assist and or ignore drug operations or face other consequences such as death of a family member.

The active bribe achieves two purposes. It allows the cartels to achieve their tactical mission and forcibly corrupts individuals which can be beneficial in future operations. A shadow government is formed when cartel leadership, either themselves or through their cadre or enforcers, using bribes or threats, allow the established government to remain in place as long as they allow the cartel's operations to continue. This method of control, using bribes, is usually found at local and state levels. Infiltration is another method that currently plagues the Mexican government. Infiltration, is widespread, the insurgents can not only obtain information about government plans and impending actions but also expand their influence by exercising de facto control over parts of the population."[88] Infiltration allows the cartels to remain in power and forgoes the need to topple the existing government.

Political cadre also perform positive tasks to win the support of the population and despite their much publicized use of brutal violence. The cartels have recognized the value of providing goods and essential services to the local population to gain their support. For instance, the Gulf Cartel has been known to, donate food, bicycles, clothing, and toys to Nuevo Laredo residents, while drug kingpins throw festivals for the residents of their strongholds. In many cases, these overtures are met with a receptive audience. Joaquin _El Chapo' Guzman, one of the leaders of the Sinaloa Cartel, is the subject of admiring narcorridos, or folk songs, that tout his generosity and his ability to elude the authorities."[89] These benefits allow the cartels to win popularity among the poor and or lower class without using violence to silence those who oppose them.

71

The Auxiliaries

As active sympathizers, the auxiliaries perform crucial services for an insurgent organization, however, they do not participate in any operations. The two types of support and insurgent organization receives from its auxiliaries are categorized as active and passive support. Active support is the most crucial to the insurgency since in encompasses, ―those who are willing to make sacrifices and risk personal harm by either joining the movement or providing the insurgents with intelligence information, concealment, shelter, hiding places for arms and equipment, medical assistance, guides, and liaison agents.‖[90] Passive support is also a valuable commodity for insurgents. Passive supporters are, ―unwilling to provide material assistance and . . . are not apt to betray or otherwise impede the insurgents.‖[91] Auxiliaries are active supporters by providing essential information and intelligence about the forces conducting counterinsurgency operations.

Auxiliaries create an advantage for the insurgent groups by providing the environment necessary to be successful. In the Mexican narco-insurgency, auxiliaries provide lookouts and manual labor in areas where the cartels produce, manufacture, transport, and sell their product. An example of how the auxiliaries are employed in Mexico was reported by the Mexico City‗s Reforma newspaper in 2007. The report stated that La Familia, ―began to sign up workers to establish a presence in Guanajuato, which is adjacent to Michoacan.‖[92] These workers met with a man known as ―The Lawyer,‖ who brokered arrangements with, ―municipal authorities in Salvatierra, Coroneo, Moroleon, and Uriangato, as well as with agents from the now-extinct Federal

72

Investigative Agency (AFI) in Uriangato and Salamnanca."[93] These new recruits then served as lookouts who would, ―alert the La Familia to military and police movements."[94]

The Mass Base

The largest element of an insurgency is the mass base which consists of individuals which the insurgents recruit from. Those within the mass base provide the insurgency with what is known as popular support. Although most of the base provides some form of passive support to the insurgency, members of the base can drift between being a regular member of society to a combatant (foot soldier) and or auxiliary member. In terms of recruitment, O'Neill breaks down the masses further into two separate categories, intelligentsia and the masses. The intelligentsia or intellectuals, ―constitute the principal source for recruitment to both high-and middle-level leadership positions (i.e., commanders of guerrilla units, terrorist networks, and political cadres)."[95]

The mass base is made up of the lower class of the population who face some type of economic or political disparities. O'Neill observes that, ―The larger the group that feel relatively deprived, the greater the possibilities for mobilizing the mass support and sustaining a widespread insurgency."[96] Manwaring notes that the root causes of gang activity in Central American and Mexico are similar in the fact that the majority of, ―[gang] members grow up in marginal areas within minimal access to basic social services; high levels of youth unemployment, compounded by insufficient access to educational and other public benefits; overwhelmed, ineffective, and often corrupt police and justice systems; easy access to weapons; dysfunctional families; and high levels of intra-familial and intra-community violence,"[97] These conditions make the masses more susceptible to recruitment for the cartels cause.

73

This type of environment provides a rich recruiting area for the drug cartels to hire or attract members to support their cause. The gangs, who are supported and act as auxiliaries for the cartels, provide these troubled youth with an opportunity to improve their lives, earn a pay check, and join an organization that excepts them for their behavior. The cartels, unlike most of Mexican society which refuses to give them a job unless it's working in the inhumane conditions of the factories, welcome them openly. O'Neill comments in his book that, "the most immediate reason for a disgruntled individual to join an organization is to increase his options for attaining the things he values or desires."[98] As discussed early, the history of Mexico dating back to the root causes found in the Mexican Revolution of 1910 helps to create a mass base that values all the opportunities the narco-insurgency can provide them. This environment provides the cartels with an endless supply of recruits and supporters.

The Scope of the Network

An insurgency will find it difficult to achieve its strategic and operational goals without the establishment of a strong support network. The network is defined as, "a series of direct and indirect ties from one actor to a collection of others. Insurgents use technological, economic, and social means to recruit partners into their organizations."[99] The network is not only good for recruiting from the population, but, finding internal and external support vital to maintaining the momentum needed to achieve the insurgent leaders goals. Due to the complexity of the network, compounded by modern technology such as the internet, it is almost impossible to understand the limits and scope of an insurgency network in today's counterinsurgency fight.

Similar to Mao's phases of insurgency, gangs evolve and extend the network. The evolution of gangs within the network is categorized as first, second, and third Generation gangs. In his article, *A Contemporary Challenge to State Sovereignty: Gangs and other Illicit Transnational Criminal Organizations in Central America, El Salvador, Mexico, Jamaica, and Brazil,* Max Manwaring describes each generation as:

First Generation: Traditional street gangs that focus on turf protection to gain petty cash. Ideology is mostly centered on gang loyalty. Criminal enterprise is largely opportunistic and individual in scope.

Second Generation: Organized for business and commercial gain, these gangs have a more centralized leadership that tends to focus on drug trafficking and market protection. They use violence as a political interference to negate enforcement efforts directed against them by police, national and local security organizations, and other competition. As these gangs develop broader, market-focused, and sometimes overtly political agendas to improve their market share and revenues, they may overtly challenge state security and sovereignty.

Third Generation: Encompassing the activities of both first and second generation gangs, third generation gangs expand their geographical bounds, as well as their commercial and political objectives. This political action is intended to provide security and freedom of movement for gang activities. As a consequence, the third-generation gang and its leadership challenge the legitimate state monopoly on the exercise of political control and the use of violence within a given geographical area. The gang leader, then, acts much like a warlord, insurgent leader, or a drug baron. The objectives for a third generation gang are to (1) neutralize, control, dispose, or replace an incumbent

75

government, (2) to control parts of a targeted country or sub-regions within a country and create autonomous enclaves that are sometimes called criminal free states or para-states, and 3) in doing so, radically change the authoritative allocation of values (governance) in a targeted society to those of criminal leaders.[100]

The reason this research highlights the evolution of gangs from a small town street gang to gangs supporting a full blown cartel driven insurgency is to show the complexity and reach of the network of the Mexican narco-insurgency. The scope of an insurgency refers to the amount of members that either fill key positions or actively support the movement. Originating from Mexico the shipment of narcotics reaches into every town in North and Central America, ultimately interconnecting each gang. The money trail and return profit can then be traced to either a small time narcotics producer within the U.S. or Canada, but experts agree that the majority of the more harmful narcotics such as cocaine and methamphetamines are produced in Mexico.

When analyzing the narco-insurgency two dynamics should alarm government officials in the U.S. and Mexico. The first alarming capability of the cartels is their overwhelming financial power. Second, is the complexity and reach of the network and organization. The network of the drug insurgency reaches into every major city and small town within the U.S. and Mexico. Within Mexico the network of the drug cartels almost effects every aspect of daily life. In Mexico, experts estimate that nearly, –85 percent of legitimate businesses are involved in some manner with La Familia."[101] This is an impressive and alarming figure since La Familia is only one of the many cartels that are operating within Mexico.

If given the opportunity and if it is economically feasible, the Mexican drug cartels will eventually extend their operations throughout the world, basically, wherever there is a demand for drugs, the cartels will be there to provide the supply. Exporting the same techniques and ideology worldwide, the drug trade will attract individuals who desire to improve their financial and social status by acting as narcotics distribution points further extending the range and influence of the drug insurgency. The spread of narcotics trafficking will eventually, if not already, threaten the legitimacy of every government, worldwide.

Chapter Four Conclusions

In summary, the situation within Mexico is an insurgency. To review, let us first take a look at our definition of insurgency. This research identified an insurgency as ‑an organization that possess the capability to use violence and the necessary resources to wage a protracted struggle, whose strategic objective is focused on delegitimizing the control of an established government in attempts to split away from and or overthrow the ruling party."

The beginnings of this protracted struggle against the Mexican government stem from the lack of social and economic improvements that the oppressed, lower working class experienced during the time of the Mexican Industrial Revolution. The need for social and economic reforms, that fueled the revolution is still present in Mexican society today, however, the many members of this social cause have turned from pursing political avenues for reform and have instead found a new remedy joining the cartels. The solution to poverty and harsh working conditions within Mexico is provided by a host of drug cartels who produce, manufacture, and distribute narcotics for profit.

77

The individual Mexican sees job opportunity and stability in the narcotics industry. He finds cohesion among his gang members and is happy to actively support the cartel operations in any role. The drug cartels recognize that in order to achieve their own economic goals through the narcotics industry, they will need the support of the population for recruitment, labor, and safe heavens. By combining these two causes, economic gain for the cartels and economic and social stability for the masses, the cartels have created an ideal environment, ripe for a narco-insurgency.

For those who are skeptical and see the narcotics industry as merely a law enforcement issue, the fact is that when dissected, the Mexican narco-insurgency represents all the characteristics and dynamics of insurgency as outlined and defined by the U.S. Army's Counterinsurgency doctrine, FM 3-24, as well as analysis and research by renowned insurgency experts. The drug cartels within Mexico have developed a system of organizations and complex networks to maximize their profits and violently defend their territory. Elements of the cartel organizations represent those found in historical insurgencies and many of the causes, ideologies, and objectives are similar, if not the same.

The political aspirations of the narco-insurgency threaten the legitimacy of the Mexican government in many different ways. First, it threatens the government with violence. Each of the drug cartels, through the profits gained from the sales of narcotics, is heavily armed and willing to employ or use violence against any threat or perceived threat, to their territory or operations. Many of the cartels employ enforcer gangs who exist solely to ensure the wishes and demands of the cartel leadership are fulfilled and their possessions are secure.

Second, the cartels delegitimize the Mexican government by providing employment and essential services to the population. In areas that the Mexican government is weak and unable to provide those services to the population is where the cartels have the most leverage and are the strongest. Inserting themselves as the leadership, voice, and protector of the people, the cartels easily gain the support of the population.

Third, the Mexican drug cartels have created a shadow government by infiltrating and bribing officials and employees within the Mexican government. This shadow government is able to influence political decisions and predict law enforcement activities and military operations targeting their drug trafficking and cartel personnel.

In Chapter 5 this research will provide possible solutions and recommendations to reduce the capabilities and influence of the cartels and perhaps stiffen the growth of the narco-insurgency raging in Mexico.

---

[1]Jack Bauer, ―The Battles on the Rio Grande: Palo Alto and Resaca de la Palma, 8-9 May 1846," in *America's First Battles 1776- 1965,* ed. Charles E. Heller and William A. Stofft (Lawrence, KS: University Press of Kansas, 1986), 57.

[2]Ibid.

[3]Ibid., 58.

[4]Ibid.

[5]Ibid.

[6]Martin C. Needler, *Mexican Politics: The Containment of Conflict* (Westport: Praeger Publisher, 1995), 3.

[7]Michael C. Meyer and William L. Sherman, *The Course of Mexican History,* 2nd ed. (Oxford: Oxford University Press, 1983), 458.

[8]Ibid.

[9]Needler, 3.

[10]Meyer and Sherman, 459.

[11]Ibid.

[12]Ibid., 461.

[13]Ibid., 483.

[14]Ibid.

[15]Ibid., 488.

[16]Ibid.

[17]Ibid., 490.

[18]Ibid., 491.

[19]Ibid., 431.

[20]Ibid., 453.

[21]Ibid., 470.

[22]Ibid., 495.

[23]Ibid., 498.

[24]Ibid., 552.

[25]Max G. Manwaring, *A "New" Dynamic in the Western Hemisphere Security Environment: The Mexican Zetas and Other Private Armies* (Carlisle, PA: Strategic Studies Institute, U.S. Army War College, 2008), 4.

[26]Ibid., 5.

[27]Ibid.

[28]Needler, 52.

[29]Ibid., 53.

[30]Ibid., 58.

[31]Ibid.

[32]Ibid.

[33]Ibid., 40.

[34]Daniel Levy and Gabriel Szekely, *Mexico: Paradoxes of Stability and Change*, 2d. ed., rev. and updated (Boulder, CO: Westview Press, 1983), 208.

[35]Needler, 39.

[36]Levy and Szekely, 209.

[37]Ibid., 208.

[38]Ibid., 209.

[39]George W. Grayson, *La Familia Drug Cartel: Implications for U.S. - Mexican Security* (Carlisle, PA: Strategic Studies Institute, U.S. Army War College, 2010), ix.

[40]Ibid.

[41]U.S. Department of the Army, Field Manual (FM) 3-24, *Counterinsurgency* (Washington, DC: Government Printing Office, 2006), 1-1.

[42]Ibid.

[43]Bard E. O'Neill, *Insurgency and Terrorism: From Revolution to Apocalypse,* 2nd ed. (Dullus: Potomac Books, 2005), 15.

[44]David Galula, *Counterinsurgency Warfare: Theory and Practice* (Westport: Praeger Security International, 1964), 1.

[45]Ibid., 2.

[46]U.S. Department of the Army, FM 3-24, *Counterinsurgency,* 1-10.

[47]Ibid., 1-14.

[48]Ibid.

[49]Ibid.

[50]Ibid.

[51]Ibid., 1-5.

[52]Galula, 14.

[53]Ibid.

[54]O'Neill, 20.

[55]Galula, 14.

[56]Ibid.

[57]Ibid., 15.

[58]U.S. Department of the Army, FM 3-24, *Counterinsurgency*, 1-10.

[59]Ibid., 1-11.

[60]Ibid.

[61]Ibid.

[62]Ibid.

[63]Manwaring, *A "New" Dynamic in the Western Hemisphere Security Environment: The Mexican Zetas and Other Private Armies,* 11.

[64]Ibid., 9.

[65]Hal Brands, *Mexico's Narco-Insurgency and U.S. Counterdrug Policy* (Carlisle, PA: Strategic Studies Institute, U.S. Army War College, 2009), 11.

[66]Manwaring, *A "New" Dynamic in the Western Hemisphere Security Environment: The Mexican Zetas and Other Private Armies,* 18.

[67]Max G. Manwaring, *A Contemporary Challenge to State Sovereignty: Gangs and other Illicit Transnational Criminal Organizations in Central America, El Salvador, Mexico, Jamaica, and Brazil* (Carlisle, PA: Strategic Studies Institute, U.S. Army War College, 2007), 19.

[68]Manwaring, *A "New" Dynamic in the Western Hemisphere Security Environment: The Mexican Zetas and Other Private Armies*, 17.

[69]Evan Brown and Dallas D. Owens, *Drug Trafficking, Violence, and Instability in Mexico, Colombia, and the Caribbean: Implications for U.S. National Security* (Carlisle, PA: Strategic Studies Institute, U.S. Army War College, 2009), 2.

[70]Grayson, *La Familia Drug Cartel: Implications for U.S.-Mexican Security*, 41.

[71]O'Neill, 116.

[72]Grayson, *La Familia Drug Cartel: Implications for U.S.-Mexican Security,* viii.

[73]Manwaring, *A "New" Dynamic in the Western Hemisphere Security Environment: The Mexican Zetas and Other Private Armies*, 21.

[74]Ibid., 21.

[75]U.S. Department of the Army, FM 3-24, *Counterinsurgency*, 1-12.

[76]O'Neill, 116.

[77]Grayson, 25.

[78]Ibid.

[79]Ibid.

[80]Ibid., 26.

[81]U.S. Department of the Army, FM 3-24, *Counterinsurgency*, 1-12.

[82]Manwaring, *A "New" Dynamic in the Western Hemisphere Security Environment: The Mexican Zetas and Other Private Armies*, 11.

[83]Ibid., 26.

[84]Ibid., 12.

[85]Ibid.

[86]U.S. Department of the Army, FM 3-24, *Counterinsurgency*, 1-12.

[87]Ibid.

[88]O'Neill, 117.

[89]Brands, 19.

[90]O'Neill, 95.

[91]Ibid.

[92]Grayson, 20.

[93]Ibid.

[94]Ibid.

[95]O'Neill, 97.

[96]Ibid.

[97]Manwaring, *A Contemporary Challenge to State Sovereignty: Gangs and other Illicit Transnational Criminal Organizations in Central America, El Salvador, Mexico, Jamaica, and Brazil*, 22.

[98]O'Neill, 121.

[99]U.S. Department of the Army, FM 3-24, *Counterinsurgency*, 1-17.

[100]Manwaring, *A Contemporary Challenge to State Sovereignty: Gangs and other Illicit Transnational Criminal Organizations in Central America, El Salvador, Mexico, Jamaica, and Brazil*, 14.

[101]Grayson, 11.

CHAPTER 5

CONCLUSIONS AND RECOMMENDATIONS

Introduction to Chapter Five

The purpose of this research is to prove that the Mexican cartels, with support from street gangs and individuals from the lower class of Mexican society, have formed a narco-insurgency that utilizes political and social influence to achieve its strategic goals of unlimited illegal economic profits. This research will show that the causes for this insurgency are a result of long term social inequalities between the classes in Mexico. This will be done by examining historical events and long lasting social and economic issues within Mexico while framing the situation with the most current insurgency and counterinsurgency doctrine. This research will also provide recommendations for the Mexican government to consider while combating this narco-insurgency and possible support functions the U.S. can perform to aid Mexico in its fight.

Chapter 5 will first provide a summary of the findings within chapter 4 and outline what these findings mean for Mexico and the U.S. This summary will be followed by general recommendations for both governments in order to establish control over the insurgency within Mexico. These recommendations are based on the same counterinsurgency references used in chapter 4 to identify the elements and dynamics of an insurgency. After reviewing the possible courses of action for controlling the insurgency in Mexico, recommendations will be made for areas in which further study would be beneficial, based on any unanswered questions discovered during the research. Finally, chapter 5 will end with a brief statement on why an officer in the U.S. Military needs to be concerned with the situation in Mexico and its impact future missions for the military.

Summary of Chapter Four

In chapter 4 this research determined that the situation, created by the drug cartels within Mexico, is an insurgency. This was determined by defining insurgency, outlining the various dynamics and elements that make up an insurgency, and then drawing parallels between the definitions, dynamics, and elements of and insurgency and the elements and operations of the drug cartels within Mexico. To reinforce these points, a careful review of Mexican History shows how the cartels are a direct descendent of the haciendas system that evolved throughout Mexico during the Mexican Industrial Revolution. This Haciendas system not only created a oligarchy system in Mexico, where a few wealthy families control all economic and political aspects of daily life, it also created a gap between the social classes so large that it spurred the Mexican Revolution of 1910.

The Haciendas system survived the revolution and was reborn as the PRI political party that ruled Mexico throughout the majority of the 20th Century and incorporated little change to solve the social issues that angered and oppressed many Mexican families. As narcotic trafficking began to increase between the U.S. and Mexico in the second-half of the 20th Century, the haciendas were relabeled cartels, and continued the haciendas tradition of focusing on economic gains for the family and acting as a shadow government throughout their respective territories. Just as the haciendas did prior to the revolution, the cartels, using their influence and rapidly increasing financial dominance, mostly from drug trafficking, steadily began threaten the legitimacy of the central government of Mexico. By creating and providing employment opportunities within the drug trafficking operation (producing, manufacturing, smuggling, distributing, security) the cartels indentified with the lower class of Mexico and their struggle for social and economic progress that the government of Mexico as failed to provide. The drug cartels recognize that in order to achieve their own economic goals through the narcotics industry, they will need the support of the population for recruitment, labor and safe heavens. By combining these two causes, economic gain for the cartels and economic and social stability for the masses, the cartels have created an ideal environment ripe for a narco-insurgency.

The political aspirations of the narco-insurgency threaten the legitimacy of the Mexican government in many different ways. First, it threatens the government with violence. Each of the drug cartels, through the profits gained from the sales of narcotics, is heavily armed and willing to employ or use violence against any threat or perceived threat, to their territory or operations. Many of the cartels employ enforcer gangs who exist solely to ensure the wishes and demands of the cartel leadership are fulfilled and their possessions are secure.

Second, the cartels continue to delegitimize the Mexican government by providing employment and essential services to the population. The areas where the cartels have the most leverage and are the strongest happen to be those in which the Mexican government is weak and unable to provide those services to the population. Inserting themselves as the leadership, voice, and protector of the people, the cartels easily gain the support of the population.

Third, the Mexican drug cartels have created a shadow government by infiltrating and bribing officials and employees within the Mexican government. This shadow government is able to influence political decisions and predict law enforcement and military operations targeting their drug trafficking and cartel personnel.

What Does this Mean for Mexico?

The conditions within Mexico warrant immediate action since Mexico faces the ultimate threat of, ―state failure,‖ and the, ―violent imposition of a radical socioeconomic-political restructuring of the state and its governance in accordance with criminal values.‖[1] Although evidence found during this research does not conclude that Mexico is a ―failed state,‖ this research has shown that there is overwhelming evidence that criminal values have assimilated into the social, economic, and political structure of Mexico. It is possible that the oligarchy system, formed by the haciendas of the past and the cartels today, is so ingrained in Mexican society and politics, that the central government of Mexico alone does not possess the capability either to militarily, socially, and or both necessary to reverse support for the cartels in favor of the people relying on legitimate means to exist. As the cartels increase in financial and military capability it is apparent that the Mexican governments,‗ ―inability to perform the business of the state are likely to lead to the eventual erosion of its authority and legitimacy,‖ and result in the state unable to, ―control its national territory or the people in it.‖[2]

The most dangerous scenario that the Mexican government currently faces is the potential cooperation and alignment of all the various cartel‗s leadership throughout Mexico. If the Mexican government is unable to swiftly regain control over the cartels and their influence over the Mexican population, the possibility of the cartels uniting in

88

opposition to against the Mexican government, will create a force so powerful the Mexican government may find itself outmanned and outgunned. In terms of insurgency phases, the aligning of the cartels into one organization could ignite a civil war within Mexico with the results mirroring those of the 1910 Revolution.

In a report titled *A Contemporary Challenge to State Sovereignty: Gangs and Other Illicit Transnational Criminal Organizations in Central America, El Salvador, Mexico, Jamaica, and Brazil*, published in December of 2007, author Max G. Manwaring summarizes the challenges the Mexican government faces in their attempts to control the narco-insurgency:

> Those who argue that instability, chaos, and conflict are the result of poverty, injustice, corruption, and misery may well be right. We must remember, however, that individual men and women are prepared to kill and to destroy and to main, and, perhaps, to die in the process, to achieve their self determined ideological and / or commercial objectives.[3]

What Does this Mean for the United States?

U.S. officials are concerned with two major issues if the narco-insurgency within Mexico is not contained. First, if uncontained, the U.S. can expect to see an increase of drug and human trafficking, smuggling across the border, along with cartel funding going to prison and violent street gangs within the U.S. The increase of narcotics within the U.S. will have a variety of negative effects on U.S. citizens, law enforcement agencies, and drug policy.

Second there would likely be an increase in violence along the border and, over time, in every major city within the U.S. The main concern with violence is the potential of –spillover" into the U.S. as a result of opposing cartels fighting for control over territory or other narcotics related issues. The spillover of violence is already occurring to a limited degree, but would exponentially increase the negative affects the U.S. population in the states bordering Mexico, particularly those living right along the border, and the different law enforcement agencies operating within those states are currently experiencing. In turn, this would likely result in an increased state and federal spending to implement more effective strategies in an attempt to bring the situation under control along the U.S. border.

The violence growing and negative affects accompanying narco-trafficking and human smuggling in the region have already generated enough concerns that it has elicited a call from the affected state populations, law enforcement officials, and politicians alike. These local and state organizations are requesting an increase by the federal government in the execution of its responsibilities to address these security issues plus provide a military boost in security along the southwestern border, to include the Gulf of Mexico and the California coast line. As the National Guard is called into service, at an ever increasing rate, to defend the southwestern border of the U.S. a proportional increase in the need for federal military support will be needed to conduct Department of Defense Support to Civil Agencies (DSCA) missions. This increase in the National Guard's mission will also result in a significant reduction in the pool of available state, Title 32, and Title 10 support assets who are available for Homeland Defense missions, affecting the overall capability of federal forces.

Increased Flow of Narcotics and Funding

The narco-insurgency within Mexico is a threat to the United State's national security. As the research outlined earlier, gangs throughout the U.S. have increasingly turned to using the distribution of narcotics as a form of financial support for their organization. Studies have shown that, ―Mexican marijuana producers in California, the Pacific northwest, and eastern U.S. are increasingly linked to each other," and many of these groups, ―maintain their affiliation with the larger groups in California and Mexico."[4] These relationships are vital to the success of narco-trafficking. There is evidence that the Mexican cartels are also increasing their relationships with, ―prison and street gangs in the United States in order to facilitate drug trafficking within the United States as well as wholesale retail distribution of the drugs."[5] The prison and street gangs within the U.S. maintain this network based on coordination and cooperation among various operating areas for, ―moving labor and materials to various sites–even across the country–as needed."[6] This illegal network is responsible for, ―more than 90% of the cocaine sold in the United States."[7]

The Mexican cartels reportedly work with, ―multiple gangs and do not take sides in the U.S. gang conflicts," and according to the FBI, only focus on, ―wholesale distribution, leaving retail sales of illicit drugs to street gangs."[8] For example, ―in January 2006, the National Drug Intelligence Center (NDIC) reported that gangs such as the Latin Kings and Mara Salvatrucha (MS-13) buy methamphetamines from the Mexican drug cartels for distribution in the southwestern United States."[9]

The connections between the well funded narco-insurgency within Mexico and the street and prison gangs within the U.S. poses a threat that without action from the U.S. and Mexican governments, the flow of narcotics and money to criminal organizations within the U.S. will continue to increase exponentially. Street gangs within the U.S. will soon be so well funded that they create a very similar situation in U.S. cities that we see in Mexico today. Street gangs will have the funding to rival the enforcement capabilities of local and state police forces in terms of weaponry, surveillance, and manning. This will result in astronomical increases in government spending for additional law enforcement improvements and an increase in other anti-drug programs such as educational programs, rehabilitation centers, and prisons.

Increase in Violence Along the Border
and in Major U.S. Cities

The primary concern for the U.S. government officials is the safety of U.S. citizens and the local population living along the southwestern border due to the threat of spillover of violence from Mexico. These concerns were heightened by recent incidents such as the shooting on 13 March 2010 when a cartel related, gunmen killed an American consular officer and her husband, an El Paso prison guard, after they had attended a children's birthday party in Ciudad Juarez, Mexico."[10] Violence is not an uncommon event in Mexico and most American's are aware of the fact that violence has been on the increase. However, concerns were raised when on the same day an associated gunmen also, killed the husband and wounded the two children of a Mexican employee of the U.S. consulate who had attended the same party,"[11] demonstrating that politically focused tactical objectives are coordinated and incorporated in this recent spike in violence.

Spillover violence is a major concern for many American's and U.S. government officials. Drug trafficking-related violence, resulted in more than 5,100 lives lost in 2008 and 6,500 deaths in 2009," while drug trafficking-related deaths in Mexico in 2010, totaled almost 11,600, a more than 70% increase over 2009."[12] The concern for an increase in violence within the U.S. is a realistic concern for the towns located along the southwestern border. However, currently, U.S. federal officials, "deny that the increase in drug trafficking-related violence in Mexico has resulted in a significant spillover of violence into the United States," and "recognize that incidents of violence have occurred and that the potential for increased violence does exist."[13]

If evidence of "spillover" begins to appear within the U.S., the Federal and State governments will be faced with numerous decisions on how to control the situation. Increases in spending for current border security programs, additional funding for partnership programs between the U.S. and Mexico, and the possibility of addressing policy issues such as, "whether altering current drug or crime policies,"[14] may aid in reducing drug trafficking-related violence in the U.S. are a small example of some of the decisions Congress will face in the near future.

As violence within Mexico continues to increase, the U.S. government is already beginning to take more action. On 25 May 2010, in a response to rising state and local concerns over poor border security, President Obama, "authorized sending up to 1,200 National Guard troops to the U.S.–Mexico border," and on 1 August 2010, those troops began deploying to the border to, "serve for a period of one year, during which they will serve in law enforcement support roles in high-crime areas along the Southwest border."[15]

In addition to sending National Guard troops to help secure the border, the Obama Administration has introduced additional initiatives. As outlined in the FY 2011 budget request, "the Obama Administration worked with the Mexican government to develop a new four-pillar strategy," that focuses on, "(1) disrupting organized criminal groups; (2) institutionalizing the rule of law; (3) building a 21st century border; and (4) building strong and resilient communities."[16] Initiatives like these will continue to place an increasing drain on the national budget until Mexico and the U.S. have gained enough momentum to successfully reverse or minimize the growth and influence of the narco-insurgency.

Vulnerabilities of the Narco-Insurgency

In order to gage the validity of possible recommendations for combating the narco-insurgency within Mexico, this research will first reference FM 3-24, *Counterinsurgency,* to understand the vulnerabilities of an insurgency. This reference will provide guidelines that will ensure any recommendations for solutions to the narco-insurgency will be grounded in counterinsurgency or COIN doctrine. For example, one quip that is passed around during COIN discussions is, "you cannot kill your way out of an insurgency." This means that an insurgency cannot be defeated by solely focusing on the destruction of enemy combatants. Conducting a counterinsurgency requires military and law enforcement action to detain or destroy the most violent hard corps extremists within the group. However, this is only part of winning, violence will continue unless popular support for the insurgency shifts to the side of the counterinsurgent. The U.S. Army FM 3-24, *Counterinsurgency* lists eight insurgent vulnerabilities:

1. The insurgents need for secrecy

2. Inconsistencies in the mobilization message

3. The need to establish a base of operation (safe houses, narcotics factories, zones of immunity)

4. The reliance of external support (Profits from narcotics sales, weapons from the U.S.)

5. The need to obtain financial resources (Profits from narcotics sales and other

   illegal activity)

6. Internal division (cartel vs. cartel, leadership disputes within a single cartel)

7. The need to maintain momentum

8. Informants within the insurgency[17]

Of these vulnerabilities, five of them apply heavily to the narco-insurgency. The first vulnerability is the need for each cartel to establish a base of operations. Without the ability to maintain safe houses for weapons storage, factory's to manufacture narcotics, and the large ―zones of immunity‖ that are protected by violent enforcer gangs who keep law enforcement from encroaching on the cartels drug-trafficking operations, the narco-insurgency will slowly become less effective and lack organization.

Second, the reliance on external support and the need to obtain financial support are both a result of smuggling and distributing narcotics within the U.S. If the cartels are unable to make the astronomical profits they are currently collecting from narcotics sales within the U.S., their ability to finance and support the loyalties of enforcer gangs and bribes for public officials will be greatly reduced leaving them vulnerable.

The third vulnerability is the threat of internal division within the narco-insurgency and cartel leadership itself. The most common internal dispute is the constant territorial battles between the cartels. Enforcer gangs and other ‗combatants‘ within the insurgency, are responsible for ensuring the security of their zones of immunity, drug-trafficking avenues, border crossing points, and distribution areas within the U.S. from the other cartels who threaten to take over these areas for their own profit. The Mexican government must remain vigilant in keeping the cartels and their gangs separate because if these groups were to unite under one, organized leader, an overpowering, revolution type threat could emerge.

Internal division also becomes a factor during struggles for power within a single cartel organization. FM 3-24 states, ―Rifts between insurgent leaders, if identified, can be exploited. Offering amnesty of a seemingly generous compromise can also cause divisions within an insurgency and present opportunities to split or weaken it."[18] This is usually a result of subordinate members perceiving poor and or weak leadership or the process of reassigning roles amongst the cartel's upper echelons as a result of a leader being killed or captured. These internal divisions can provide cracks for law enforcement to exploit.

Finally, the threat of informants within an insurgency offers another vulnerability that law enforcement can exploit. ―Nothing is more demoralizing to insurgents than realizing that people inside their movement or trusted supporters among the public are deserting or providing information to government authorities."[19] The cartels ensure that everyone who operates within their organization fears the repercussions of being labeled an informant. Although they are usually not classified or referred to technically as ―informants," when the mass base or public loses its incentive to provide active or passive support to the insurgent (cartels), it allows law enforcement the opportunity to react to and combat insurgent activities. Winning the support of the mass base is the first sign that the counterinsurgents efforts are working.

O'Neill reinforces the idea that by eliminating external support, establishing the rule of law, and winning the support of the population create vulnerabilities of an insurgency and or narco-insurgency. O'Neill states that external support, ―is important because operatives, supplies, weapons, and other forms or aid for terrorists often come from the outside."[20] Removing the internal support for an insurgency is also a task for the counterinsurgent. O'Neill suggests that, ―internal terrorism and small scale, *urban* guerrilla attacks against soldiers and policemen are most effectively dealt with by emphasizing police work, good intelligence, and judicial sanctions."[21]

Recommendations

The narco-insurgency within Mexico, much like historical insurgencies, will require long term solutions that could possibly last decades until major improvements are apparent. ―The main targets are not pieces of territory to be seized and held but rather the insurgents themselves, as well as their supporters, sources of supply, and organization."[22] The recommendations for the Mexican government focus on exporting the vulnerabilities of a narco-insurgency. However, the long term solutions for Mexico to prevent future issues will require major social, economic, and political solutions. Indicative to counterinsurgency operations, to defeat the narco-insurgency, solutions will not only require cooperation and coordinated between Mexican law enforcement and military efforts, but a total government approach in order to win back the support of the Mexican people. ―History suggests that a government can most effectively undercut insurgencies that rely on mass support by splitting the rank and file away from the leadership through calculated reforms that address the material grievances and needs of the people."[23]

The U.S. can assist the Mexican government in many ways short of deploying U.S. Forces into the country due to the past conflicts such as the U.S. Mexican War. Support from the U.S. will consist primarily of operations north of the U.S. Mexican border and _behind the scenes' training and monetary support for the Mexican law enforcement and military.

The recommendations this research will focus on stem from the vulnerabilities of an insurgency. These recommendations are (1) eliminate the narco-insurgency's base operations,(2) Remove external support to the narco-insurgency by establishing border security between the U.S. and Mexico, (3) create internal divisions by removing narco-insurgency leadership with law enforcement efforts to create power struggles within the cartels, and (4) develop informants within the narco-insurgency organization and amongst the public by establishing the rule of law and security.

It is recommended that in order to eliminate the narco-insurgency's base of operations, Mexico must remove the external support from narcotics sales coming from the U.S., and create internal divisions within the cartels. To do this the Mexican government must focus on increasing their law enforcement and military capabilities throughout Mexico and along the border with the U.S. These capabilities will need to focus on establishing security in areas where the lack of a legitimate government presence leaves, -a vacuum in which gangs, drug cartels, leftist insurgents, the political and narco-right, and the government itself may all compete for power."[24] The efforts to extend influence into these areas will restrict and in some cases, remove the cartels ability to operate freely. Establishing a stronger presence along the border to interdict the flow of narcotics north into the U.S., and to stop the shipments of money and weapons moving south, will enable the Mexican government to slowly strangle the narco-insurgency's main supply and support lines. Increased law enforcement capabilities that successfully remove gang and cartel leadership will create power vacuums within the various

98

organizations and networks that ultimately will lead to internal divisions and disorganization.

To develop informants within the narco-insurgency and amongst the public, Mexican forces must establish security for the population and enforce the rule of law. Although security, state presence, and social and economic progress are, ―all important mutually reinforcing elements in establishing a government's authority and legitimacy, it is the rule of law and its acceptance by the people that binds them all together."[25] The rule of law is comprised of six elements: order and security, legitimacy, checks and balances, fairness, effective application, and efficiency and integrity.

By establishing the rule of law throughout Mexico, focusing especially in areas where gangs and cartels conduct drug trafficking operations without the threat of government intervention, the government will increase its legitimacy to protect the people and ultimately win their support against violent narco-insurgency organizations. Once the people feel secure, and trust the established rule of law within Mexico, those who support the government will provide the intelligence needed by law enforcement and military units to conduct effective counterinsurgency operations against the cartels.

Support from the United States

The U.S. can assist Mexico in its counterinsurgency operations by continuing with programs such as the Merida Initiative. The Merida Initiative was signed into law by President Bush on 30 June 2008, as a response to the situation within Mexico. The Merida Initiative was a, ―3-year, $1.4 billion counternarcotics package," that aimed at using, ―U.S. money, training, and equipment to strengthen Mexico's military and law enforcement agencies, thereby giving them the capacity to take a hold the initiative in the fight against the cartels."[26] The emphasis of the Merida Initiative focuses on the insurgency's vulnerability of external support by emphasizing, "interdiction and enforcement initiatives," and the, "supply-side approach to the drug trade."[27] The Merida Initiative encompasses the counterinsurgency approach by also providing, "domestic treatment and prevention initiatives, source-country development programs, and other alternative strategies."[28]

The success of the Merida Initiative is hopeful based on similar operations within Columbia to weaken the control of the FARC by establishing the rule of law within the country. Between 2000 and 2008, the U.S. spent $238.9 million to, "promote the rule of law, judicial reform, and complementary capacity building in Columbia."[29] The effort was an interagency effort by the U.S. with, "the work being supervised by the United States Agency for International Development (USAID) and the Department of Justice (DOJ)"[30] Similar to Columbia, one issue plaguing the Mexican justice system is its low conviction rate. Within Columbia, "criminal cases are now resolved in 75 percent less time (weeks and months instead of years), and over 60 percent of cases formally charged are resulting in convictions, compared to with 3 percent under the old system."[31] With these improvements in the justice system and other security programs with the support of the U.S., the Mexican government will slowly begin shifting the support of the population away from the gangs and cartels. As this support shifts in favor of the Mexican governments' counterinsurgency operations, tolerance for the cartels will decrease and the cartels influence will slowly be degraded to manageable levels.

For Future Study

During this research the two issues were heavily debated amongst experts and advocates who see the situation within Mexico and the U.S. as something that requires drastic measures. First, is the construction of a barrier along the southwestern border of the U.S. to facilitate American law enforcement and border patrol agencies in their operations to interdict drug and human smuggling along the border. The effectiveness of this barrier compared to its overall cost is an issue that warrants additional research and may lead to other possible solutions for interdicting narco-trafficking between the U.S. and Mexico.

The second heavily debated topic centers on the effects that legalizing marijuana and or drugs within the U.S. will do for the War on Drugs. If research were to determine if in fact marijuana and or other harmless and natural drugs should be made legal, studies into the distribution of profits gained from taxing drug sales and production would be vital. Using money gained from the taxation of marijuana sales, the government could fuel much more vital operations and or initiatives to interdict terrorist operations and or dangerous narcotics being transported from Mexico into the U.S.

The U.S. Military Officer and the Narco-insurgency

The importance for today's U.S. Military officer to understand the situation along the border is critical. As the U.S. slowly retrogrades from fighting insurgencies in Iraq and Afghanistan and the military is forced to conduct its traditional post-conflict downsizing, the need for the American military to apply its counterinsurgency knowledge closer to home is quickly becoming a reality. The difference in this fight along the southwestern border and within the country of Mexico to those of Iraq and Afghanistan is in the role of Title 10 forces who will transition from leading to supporting. Federal military support will be called to assist National Guard units operating along the border in order to secure the American public.

Those U.S. Military personnel who do deployed into Mexico will, at most, serve as advisors and trainers to the Mexican military. Their ability to understand not only the elements and dynamics of an insurgency but the unique characteristics of a narco-insurgency will be vital to their success. Insights, such as this research, can provide perspectives and, ―reveal critical social, economic, and political problems that it [the government] must address, as well as provide insights into the feasibility of various antidotes."[32] U.S. Military officers will also require the necessary skills and knowledge to conduct a Department of Defense Support to Civilian Authorities (DSCA) mission. The need for the U.S. Military to provide this training to company and field grade level officers is vital to the success of the mission and maintaining the positive relationship between the American public and it's military.

---

[1]Max G. Manwaring, *A Contemporary Challenge to State Sovereignty: Gangs and other Illicit Transnational Criminal Organizations in Central America, El Salvador, Mexico, Jamaica, and Brazil* (Carlisle, PA: Strategic Studies Institute, U.S. Army War College, 2007), 19.

[2]Ibid.

[3]Ibid., 17.

[4]Colleen W. Cook, *Mexico's Drug Cartels,* RL34215 (Washington, DC: Congressional Research Service, 2007), 5.

[5]Ibid., 9.

[6]Ibid., 8.

[7]Clare Ribando Seelke and Kristin M. Finklea, R41349, *U.S. -Mexican Security Cooperation: the Merida Initiative and Beyond* (Washington, DC: Congressional Research Service, 2011), 6.

[8]Cook, 9.

[9]Ibid.

[10]Clare Ribando Seelke, RL32724, *Mexico-U.S. Relations: Issues for Congress* (Washington, DC: Congressional Research Service, 2010), 10.

[11]Ibid.

[12]Seelke and Finklea, 7.

[13]Seelke, 11.

[14]Seelke and Finklea, 10.

[15]Ibid.

[16]Ibid., 2.

[17]U.S. Department of the Army, Field Manual (FM) 3-24, *Counterinsurgency* (Washington, DC: Government Printing Office, 2006), 1-17.

[18]Ibid., 19.

[19]Ibid.

[20]Bard E. O'Neill, *Insurgency and Terrorism: From Revolution to Apocalypse,* 2d ed., rev. (Dullus: Potomac Books, 2005), 160.

[21]Ibid., 159.

[22]Ibid., 162.

[23]Ibid., 172.

[24]Manwaring, *A Contemporary Challenge to State Sovereignty: Gangs and other Illicit Transnational Criminal Organizations in Central America, El Salvador, Mexico, Jamaica, and Brazil,* 17.

[25]Gabriel Marcella, *Democratic Governance and the Rule of Law: Lessons from Colombia* (Carlisle, PA: Strategic Studies Institute, U.S. Army War College, 2009), 8.

[26]Hal Brands, *Mexico's Narco-Insurgency and U.S. Counterdrug Policy* (Carlisle, PA: Strategic Studies Institute, U.S. Army War College, 2009), 8.

[27]Ibid., 9.

[28]Ibid.

[29]Marcella, 36.

[30]Ibid.

[31]Ibid.

[32]O'Neill, 166.

BIBLIOGRAPHY

Books

Bauer, Jack. ―The Battles on the Rio Grande: Palo Alto and Resaca de la Palma, 8-9 May 1846." In *America's First Battles 1776- 1965*, edited by Charles E. Heller and William A. Stofft, 57-81. Lawrence, KS: University Press of Kansas, 1986.

Brown, Evan, and Dallas D. Owens. *Drug Trafficking, Violence, and Instability in Mexico, Colombia, and the Caribbean: Implications for U.S. National Security.* Carlisle, PA: Strategic Studies Institute, U.S. Army War College, 2009.

Creswell, John W., *Qualitative Inquiry and Research Design: Choosing Among Five Approaches*, 2d ed. Thousand Oaks: Sage Publications, Inc., 2007.

Galula, David. *Counterinsurgency Warfare: Theory and Practice.* Westport: Praeger Security International, 1964.

Levy, Daniel and Gabriel Szekely, *Mexico: Paradoxes of Stability and Change*, 2nd. ed. Boulder, CO: Westview Press, 1983.

Meyer, Michael C. and Sherman, William L. *The Course of Mexican History,* 2nd ed. Oxford: Oxford University Press, 1983.

Needler, Martin C. *Mexican Politics: The Containment of Conflict.* Westport: Praeger Publisher, 1995.

O'Neill, Bard E. *Insurgency and Terrorism: From Revolution to Apocalypse,* 2d ed. Dullus: Potomac Books, 2005.

Periodicals

Gentile, Gian P. ―Our coin doctrine removes the enemy from the essence of war." *Armed Forces Journal* (2006). http://www.armedforcesjournal.com/2008/01/3207722 (accessed 3 January 2001).

Johnson, Alex. ―In Mexico's drug wars, fears of U.S. front." *MSNBC*, 9 March, 2009. http://www.msnbc.msn.com/id/29516551/ (accessed 17 October 2010).

Los Angeles Times. ―Mexico Under Siege: The drug war at our doorstep." http://projects.latimes.com/mexico-drug-war/#/its-a-war (accessed 17 October 2010).

Moore, Solomon. ―How U.S. Became Stage for Mexican Drug Feud." *The New York Times*, 8 December, 2009. http://www.ny times.com/2009/12/09/us/09border.html (accessed 17 October 2010).

New York Times. ―Mexican Drug Trafficking," 21 October, 2010. http://topics.nytimes. com/top/news/international/countriesandterritories/mexico/drug_trafficking/index .html?scp=1&sq=mexican%20drug%20cartels&st=cse (accessed 17 October 2010).

Stevenson, Mark. ―Clinton: Mexican Drug Cartels Like ‗Insurgency'." *Fox News*, 9 September 2010. http://www.foxnews.com/world/2010/09/08/mexican-mayor-killed-marines-arrest-suspects-massacre-migrants/ (accessed 17 October 2010).

Wilkinson, Tracy. ―A Top Salavdoran Ex-guerrilla Commander Advised Mexico's Conservative President." *Los Angeles Times*, 22 October 2010. http://www.la times.com/news/nationworld/world/la-fg-mexico-guru-20101023,0,7109037.story (accessed 17 October 2010).

Government Documents

Brands, Hal. *Mexico's Narco-Insurgency and U.S. Counterdrug Policy.* Carlisle, PA: Strategic Studies Institute, U.S. Army War College, 2009.

Cook, Colleen W. RL34215, *Mexico's Drug Cartels.* Washington, DC: Congressional Research Service, 2007.

Federation of American Scientists. ―About FAS." http://www.fas.org/ (accessed 17 October 2010).

Grayson, George W. *La Familia Drug Cartel: Implications for U.S. - Mexican Security.* Carlisle, PA: Strategic Studies Institute, U.S. Army War College, 2010.

Lauder, Matthew A. *Religion and Resistance: Examining the Role of Religion in Irregular Warfare.* Toronto: Defense R&D Canada, 2009.

Manwaring, Max G. *A Contemporary Challenge to State Sovereignty: Gangs and other Illicit Transnational Criminal Organizations in Central America, El Salvador, Mexico, Jamaica, and Brazil.* Carlisle, PA: Strategic Studies Institute, U.S. Army War College, 2007.

―――. *A "New" Dynamic in the Western Hemisphere Security Environment: The Mexican Zetas and Other Private Armies.* Carlisle, PA: Strategic Studies Institute, U.S. Army War College, 2008.

Marcella, Gabriel. *Democratic Governance and the Rule of Law: Lessons from Colombia.* Carlisle, PA: Strategic Studies Institute, U.S. Army War College, 2009.

Seelke, Clare Ribando, and Kristin M. Finklea. R41349, *U.S.-Mexican Security Cooperation: the Merida Initiative and Beyond.* Washington, DC: Congressional Research Service, 2011.

————. RL32724, *Mexico-U.S. Relations: Issues for Congress.* Washington, DC: Congressional Research Service, 2010.

Strategic Studies Institute. "About Us." http://www.strategicstudiesinstitute.army.mil/ (accessed 3 January 2011).

U.S. Department of the Army. Field Manual (FM) 3-24, *Counterinsurgency.* Washington, DC: Government Printing Office, 2006.

U.S. Department of Defense. Joint Publication (JP) 3-27, *Homeland Defense.* Washington, DC: Government Printing Office, 2007.

————. Joint Publication (JP) 3-28, *Civil Support.* Washington, DC: Government Printing Office, 2007.

The White House. *National Defense Strategy, June 2008.* Washington, DC: Government Printing Office.